AMERICAN GUIDE TO
U.S. COINS

AMERICAN GUIDE TO U.S. COINS

By Charles F. French

& Leslie Zeller

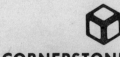

CORNERSTONE LIBRARY
Published by Simon & Schuster
New York

CONTENTS

Preface

Charles French was my mentor. Nearly thirty years ago, when the information explosion did not yet exist, and I was a rank numismatic neophyte, his modest shop in upstate New York was a gathering place for those of us hungry for information on the numismatic issues of our country; not "how many" of a certain piece were originally minted, but just why, in the real world, could you find any number of red uncirculated half-cents of 1855, and not a single specimen of 1853 in like condition.

The real reasons for that, and a thousand other puzzles to our fledgling generation would be offered swiftly and accurately by a smiling man with a great, booming voice, "Charlie" French. He was always there, an indefatigable storyteller, and awful punster, to set the novice straight as he saw it. And see it he did, from the time of the pioneer American dealers such as the Chapmans, just after World War I to the days of the super-dealers only a couple of years ago when Charlie passed on.

I have changed very little in the prose of this edition so that the flavor of the man lives on. But market conditions, like time and tide, change constantly, and over three thousand corrections are in order. So it is to be hoped that this, the latest edition of THE AMERICAN GUIDE TO U.S. COINS is the most accurate available.

LESLIE ZELLER

AMERICAN GUIDE TO
U.S. COINS

Part One:

SOME HISTORY AND SOME ADVICE

INTRODUCTION:
A BRIEF HISTORY
OF AMERICAN NUMISMATICS

The discovery in 1843 of the celebrated 1804 silver dollar is one of the earliest indications we have of interest in American numismatics. While there is a great deal of discussion regarding this coin's authenticity, it is generally agreed that the earliest were struck with the revision of Mint operations during the 1836-40 period. From 1858 on, the United States Mint struck proofs for collectors and, although not many of these were issued, this shows that there was numismatic interest at that time.

The middle of the nineteenth century saw great interest in revising our coinages. It was the policy of the Mint to strike "trial" or experimental coins, and there appeared such unusual denominations as two-cent, three-cent, and twenty-cent pieces, none of which met with much popularity in circulation. They therefore were ultimately discontinued. Trial pieces became very popular with collectors in the 1860s and 1870s and it is possible that a good many of these were struck purely for the delight of the collector. Usually only a dozen or so patterns were needed, but quantities up to five hundred of some were struck.

The latter part of the nineteenth century saw the start of the American Numismatic Association and the publishing of America's first monthly magazine devoted exclusively to numismatics. Students came into being who ardently studied their particular field, and many books of value were published towards the end of the century. The majority of these books were about cents and half cents; other topics covered were Colonial coins, half dimes, quarters, halves, and dollars. The continuing popularity of large cents explains why there were so many publications about these interesting coins.

The following authors were pioneers in their subjects and paved the way for the many publications that have since appeared: Ebenezer Gilbert, Ed Frossard, Sylvester Crosby, W.W. Hays, Thomas Elder, F.W. Doughty, George H. Clapp, H.R. Newcomb, H.P. Newlin, D.W. Valentine, A.W. Browning, J.W. Haseltine, M.L. Beistle, Dr. M.W. Dickeson, Dr. Edward Maris, Philip Nelson, Sydney P. Noe, Carl Wurzbach, and Miller-Ryder.

There is no accurate record of the number of collectors in those days, but I would estimate that they must have numbered between three and five hundred. There were no "coin boards" or plastic holders. Collectors had to improvise. The wealthier had wooden cabinets built, fitted with velvet-lined trays; others lined cigar boxes with velvet and placed their coins in these. Many a pleasant hour was spent going over coin collections, pointing out prized pieces to friends. Trading and exchanging coins with fellow numismatists became the thing to do.

Probably the first coin holders to become popular were the small round cardboard "pill" boxes manufactured by T. James Clarke of Jamestown, New York. Mr. Clarke, being a well-known collector of large cents, sold these boxes as containers for large cents, for they were just the right size. Collectors would put cotton in the bottom of the box, place the coin in it, and write its description on the cover.

At the beginning of the twentieth century, coin collecting was a hobby only for the few deeply interested in the subject. There were perhaps several thousand collectors at this time. They formed a national "clique" deeply interested in coin research, finding new rarities and new varieties. One of the first boons to the hobby was the issue of several million Columbian half dollars during the World's Fair in Chicago in 1892. This was the first coin struck in America commemorating an event and offered for sale to all. It opened the eyes of the public to the possibilities of coin collecting and showed how it could be interesting and even profitable. Collectors fondly kept those commemorative memoirs of the World's Fair. The success of this first commemorative encouraged the issue of many more from 1915 on and while these helped keep the hobby active, they did not materially increase the number of collectors.

In the middle of the 1920s, the largest coin dealer was B. Max Mehl, who used the radio and national newspaper advertising to foster the sale of his new and excellent coin book, the "Star Rare Coin Encylopedia." This book gave collectors buying prices for all United States coins and also had many articles of interest on coins from all parts of the world, plus information about coin collecting. The book was a truly educational volume. It cost him thousands of dollars to advertise, but since he sold hundreds of thousands of books at a dollar each, we suspect he didn't lose any money. Mehl's coin book helped give the public a new awareness of numismatics, an awareness that was so far-reaching that even today we occasionally hear his great slogan, "I'll give fifty dollars for a 1913 Liberty-Head nickel." In fact, it was B. Max Mehl who made the 1913 nickel such a popular and desirable coin.

Up to the depression of 1929-33, coin values had gradually increased, as had new coin collectors. I would estimate that in 1930 there were probably ten thousand coin collectors in the USA—many of them hard-pressed for money due to the depression. During those years collectors' coins could be purchased very reasonably. With the return of prosperity, a new stimulus came to numismatics. The many new issues of commemorative coins in 1935 and 1936 caused coin speculation on a large scale for the first time. Easy profits brought the speculator into the field. Commemorative prices skyrocketed, and all United States coins were affected; values rose substantially. As might have been expected, when commemoratives crashed in 1937-38 many of the "fast-buck boys" lost interest in the hobby.

The first auction sales took place very early in the nineteenth century. There were only one or two well-known coin auctioneers at that time. Toward the latter part of the 1930s, many new auctioneers went into the business. I still have a letter from a well-known dealer and auctioneer, Thomas Elder, bemoaning the fact that with all the auctions being conducted and coins being offered, prices would surely crash and coins become valueless. If only he had lived to see what has occurred and how greatly the hobby has grown!

In the beginning of the 1940s, many coin minded people were confident of the future of numismatics. They reasoned that if the number of collectors continued to increase and there were no more coins to be had, prices would rise. They began accumulating uncirculated rolls of current coins against future demands. These investors would secure the rolls at their banks, or send away to dealers who specialized in this kind of business, and store them in safe deposit boxes. Uncirculated rolls were excellent investments, for how could one lose? At worst, the coins could be deposited in their bank at face value. Those who held these rolls long enough made small fortunes.

During the depression, the Whitman Publishing Company first nationally put on the market an attractive, reasonably priced series of coin boards designed to encourage new collectors. They showed the novice what and how to collect, mostly, from his pocket change, and were offered throughout the United States in many kinds of stores. They steadily increased the number of coin collectors and are still a major factor in encouraging new ones.

Another great boon to numismatics was the resumption of the manufacture of proof sets in 1936 by the United States Mint in Philadelphia. Not many proofs were sold from 1936 through 1942 and none were made during the war years of 1943-49. The record of the number of proof sets coined from 1950 on clearly indicates their increasing popularity. When one considers that there were 51,386 sets coined in 1950 and 3,950,762 in 1964, the answer is obvious as to the interest in coin collecting as a hobby.

Many people ask "Why do collectors like proof sets?" The first answer occurs when you consider the care and accuracy with which they are coined, and also their beautiful mirror-like finish. Second, there is a great appeal to collecting a series. Third, their value has constantly increased and they have been an excellent investment in the past.

Probably one of the greatest boons in recent years has been the introduction of coin newspapers, weekly and biweekly publications that reach all coin collectors, dealers and even people who are only slightly interested in coins. Shortly after the first issue of the coin newspapers, their circulation was nearly a hundred thousand; this was a great surprise to all "old time" numismatists, many of whom did not realize how wide the interest in coins had become.

A recent innovation is the advertised "bid" and "ask" prices, by dealers, of uncirculated rolls, proof sets, and commemoratives. These give the collector and investor an idea of current value. Weekly published "trends" give an idea of how the market on all regularly issued coins is faring. For today's prices change very rapidly, sometimes up and sometimes down. Those interested are coin collectors of all classes, beginners, Whitman board collectors, speculators, investors, regular collectors, dealers, and students. The majority are new to the hobby and have a great deal to learn.

The law of supply and demand governs prices. When the supply is short and demand great, values are bound to increase. When certain pieces rise to very high prices, a great many small collectors are frozen out of the market for these particular coins. However, this only applies to coins that run well into the thousands of dollars per coin.

The American Numismatic Association conducts a national convention once a year in August held in various cities of the United States. Fifteen years ago, coin clubs began springing up throughout our country. Today there are very few cities of respectable size that do not have their own clubs. They meet, usually once a month, conduct their business meetings, have talks on numismatics, occasionally conduct a club auction, buy and sell coins, and even have displays. They are always interested in gaining new members.

The large number of collectors and clubs has encouraged the forming of regional associations and you will find that these associations cover practically the entire country. Joined by clubs and collectors in their regional territory, these associations hold either one or two conventions per year. Many have auction sales conducted during their convention and a bourse where dealers from all over the United States congregate to offer their coins for sale. Collectors are encouraged to display their collections and are awarded prizes for their efforts on a competitive basis.

Numismatics today is well organized. Since its start, in 1891 the American Numismatic Association has grown slowly and steadily until its membership is well over thirty thousand. Under this parent organization come the regional associations and then the local coin clubs. In addition to the above, there is the American Numismatic Society in New York City, which maintains an outstanding museum of rare coins. The society has a remarkable library and issues many new publications, devoting its efforts to research.

1.

EARLY

AMERICAN COINS

Were we to transport ourselves back three centuries to the early days of Colonial America, we would find that industry was very small and that business, for the most part, was conducted by barter and trade. While the need of coins was felt, the shortage was not as important as later, when Colonial America became more industrialized and succeeded in acquiring wealth. Even so, attempts to issue coins were made.

Massachusetts experimented with its NE (New England) shillings, sixpence, and threepence. These very crude and rare coins are credited with being the first coins struck in the territories then known as the American Colonies.

Following quickly came the Willow, Oak, and Pine Tree series. Some were to find use in circulation, for in those days a coin was a coin regardless of who issued it, and the amount of metal it contained determined its value. This first series was strongly disapproved of by Charles II of England, and the coinage was stopped.

There were other very early experiments in coinage in other Colonies. The Mark Newby halfpence, struck in Dublin in 1678, was originally coined for Ireland but found its way to New Jersey. There were also the Lord Baltimore pieces for Maryland, which were coined in England and brought over for circulation here.

After these early attempts, we find little activity numismatically until the first part of the eighteenth century, when a small flurry again occurred. We have the Gloucester tokens of 1714, and the Wood or Hibernia series and Rosa Americana coins of 1722 and 1724. There were the early French Colony coppers of 1721-22; and a little earlier, the Elephant tokens of 1694. With the exception of the Gloucester tokens, of which little is known, the rest were struck in foreign lands and shipped here for use, due to the dire need. The Higley, or Granby, coppers of 1737-39 saw considerable circulation, even though they were unauthorized and coined on this continent.

As we enter the second period of inactivity, the 1767 French Colony pieces, with the exception of the 1760 Voce Populi coins, find little or no interest in "coins for America." The next and most important era commenced around the time of our embarking on the American Revolution. From this time until the opening of the first United States Mint, in 1792-93, we find innumerable varieties, experiments, in fact all types of coins. Some received recognition and actually circulated. Others should be classified as pattern or experimental pieces. Of these I shall first discuss the State cents.

New Hampshire, as early as 1776, struck coppers. As shown by their great amount of wear, they must have circulated considerably, even though very few are known. Vermont issued many varieties and quite a few cents from 1785 through 1788, and they were actively used in circulation. New York, too, issued cents from 1786 through 1787, some of which could be considered experimental pieces, others actually circulated. Connecticut probably had the most active coinage system from 1785 through 1788. All of her coins were circulated extensively. Massachusetts struck some early experimental pieces around 1776 and went into regular coinage during 1787 and 1788. New Jersey issued a wide variety of cents from 1786 through 1788. Virginia, in 1773, struck pennies and halfpennies with George III on them.

During this time, just prior to the Revolution, a wide variety of experimental coins or tokens appeared. The majority did not see circulation even though some are known to have been used. In this group we find the rare pewter pattern Continental dollars of 1776; the Nova Constellatio coppers of 1783-85-86; the

Immune Columbia pieces, the Confederatio cents; Brasher's experimental pieces, and Chalmers Annapolis (Maryland) shillings, sixpence, and threepence. Belonging here, too, are the U.S.A. Bar cents, Mott tokens, Talbot, Allum, and Lee tokens, Georgius Triumpho tokens, Auctori Plebis tokens, Kentucky tokens, Myddleton tokens, North American tokens, Pitt tokens, Rhode Island Ship tokens, and Franklin Press cents.

Now we come to what may be the forerunners of our first regular coinage, the Washington pieces. George Washington's great popularity at the end of the Revolution made it natural to want to copy the practice of foreign nations and place the head of the ruler on the obverse of the coin. There being no "ruler" of the United States, the president was the logical equivalent. If this practice had been accepted and carried out until today, we would have had a change in coin design with each president; the bust or head of each president would have appeared on our coins while he was in office. This would have been an interesting series for our coin collectors, but the many changes might very possibly have confused our coinage. (This frequent changing of coin designs did not occur in kingdoms, for the rulers were in for life.)

The practice of using Washington's head was therefore discarded and the Liberty-Head designs adopted. Many of the designs from Washington pieces, however, were adopted either partly or entirely.

The reverse of the Unity cents of 1783 is almost identical to the reverse design adopted on the wreath-type cents of 1793 and the following years. The eagle on the reverse of the various cents and half dollars is very similar to the eagle adopted for the reverse of our silver coins.

The designs of the half disme, disme, Birch cent, and silver-center cents are almost identical to the designs adopted on our coins of 1793. The Fugio cents of 1787 which actually saw circulation, while authorized by Congress, were coined privately.

You will notice that all of the above were coinages designed to fill the need of minor coins, mostly cent and half-cent sizes; this was the size that was needed most. Business requirements in larger transactions were carried on in gold Spanish-American doubloons and their fractions, English guineas, and even French louis d'or. Silver requirements were largely supplied by the masses of one-, two-, four-, and eight-real coins of Spanish America.

2.

PIRATE AND
REVOLUTIONARY MONEY

Our coasts were infested with pirates and privateers during the early days of our Colonial History. This made shipping hazardous and uncertainty was the order of the day. British, French, and particularly Spanish ships were liable to be boarded, stripped of their cargo and then sunk. With the exception of the Spaniards shipping gold and silver treasure back to Spain other cargoes usually consisted of articles sorely needed by settlers in the new world; guns, ammunitions and luxuries desired by the rich.

Gold and silver were not always in coin form for bullion was found to be more easily handled.

The Spaniards lost many ships of treasure, either through pirate raids or sunk by hurricanes. Gold coins, subjected to the action of salt water are not harmed at all, neither are rare jewels, but silver is badly affected by the corrosive action of the salt and these must be treated carefully to remove the corrosion and encrustations they acquire after centuries of lying under salt water.

During the American Revolution, the need for hard money was so great in the United States that it encouraged our authorizing private shipowners to turn "pirate." Known as privateers, these sleek fast ships roved our coast and captured any ship they could as a prize of war, placing their American crews on them and sending them to the Colonies. For the ship captains and owners this was a very lucrative business and many of the wealthy clipper ship owners of the next fifty years started out in this manner. The wealth of unobtainable material these privateers brought to the revolting Colonies was of terrific aid to the successful consummation of the war. Not only were goods brought to our shores, but a sorely needed quantity of hard money. Many English gold guineas were confiscated as they were being shipped over to the continent to pay English armies.

We must try to visualize the situation of that day in order to realize the need of this money. The early Americans had always considered hard coins the only money of real value; gold coins were used for business transactions of merit. It made no difference from what country the coins came as long as they were coins; this also applied to silver and copper. The dire needs of the war caused the individual colonies to issue paper currency, which was not looked upon with much favor.

When the Continental Congress began issuing paper currency to pay bills, their money was looked down upon and inflation swept the country to a degree that almost wrecked the war efforts. The expression "Not worth a Continental" comes to us from those days when everyone shied away from these bills. They never were redeemed and finally became of no value. For the most part, however, the earlier notes issued by the individual colonies were redeemed, but in varying percentages of their face value. To aggravate the situation further, the British resorted to counterfeiting our paper money and attempting to circulate it.

3.

GOLD DOLLARS
AND GOLDEN EAGLES

Prior to the establishment of our United States Mint, a proposal was made, in 1785, to coin five-dollar pieces, but the actual approval of our first gold pieces did not come until 1792 when Congress passed an act authorizing the coinage of eagles ($10.00), half eagles ($5.00), and quarter eagles ($2.50). The eagles were to be 247½ grains pure, 270 grains standard. Half eagles were to be 123¾ pure, 135 grains standard; quarter eagles were to be 61⅞ pure, 67½ grains standard. The standard weight included an alloy to make the coins wear better.

These gold coins were pegged to silver on a 15 to 1 ratio, namely fifteen ounces of silver to one ounce of gold, and while this ratio was all right at the time the bill was passed, by 1799 the ratio in Europe had reached 15¾ to 1, and the overvalued gold coins began to flow out of the country or were melted down to get the extra value they contained. Gold therefore disappeared from circulation, as did silver dollars.

It wasn't until June 28, 1834, that a new law reduced the weight of gold coins. From that time on, our gold pieces appeared in the new smaller size, returned to circulation, and created a new interest in and demand for gold. Gold mines profitably increased their production. Our mint first struck twenty-dollar double eagles, and experimented with fifty-dollar coins in 1849. We also find our first gold dollars appearing, closely followed by threes. The three-dollar gold piece, first coined in 1854, was never a popular coin. It was frequently linked with bad luck by the superstitious.

The quantities of gold and shortages of gold coins in the west prompted the coinage of pioneer pieces in many denominations. Privately issued and not under rigid regulations, many of these were not up to standard fineness; as late as the latter part of the 1920s these pioneer pieces were looked down upon as low-grade, undervalued coins and were redeemed by financial institutions at less than face value. Today, these low-grade coins are rare and worth high premiums, not for their gold value but for their numismatic value.

From the time shortly after the Civil War until the banking holiday in 1933, numismatic interest in collecting gold coins was not high, perhaps because of the coins' face value. Anyone who wanted to collect them could easily have secured the majority of all denominations for very little over face value, even back to 1834, when the new smaller size was adopted. A great many of the first gold pieces prior to 1804 could have been purchased for much less than their rarity should have dictated.

Proof gold coins were not popular with collectors. With the exception of the last few years, only twenty-five to forty proof gold dollars have been struck each year! Similar small quantities were coined in proofs for quarter eagles, threes, half eagles, eagles, and double eagles. The largest quantity of gold proof dollars of any year were struck in 1889, and this only amounted to 1,779 pieces! The majority of proofs struck in all denominations per year usually ran from twenty to forty specimens! Over ten times that amount or more were struck for coins in silver and copper. It is no wonder that perfect proof gold pieces bring very high prices today.

Due to the depression of 1929–33 and the uncertainty of the country's financial position, hoarding of gold coins by individuals became so common it seriously endangered our financial structure. This was one of the major reasons for the government order that all gold coins be turned in. The purpose of this order was to end hoarding and get gold back where it could do the country more good. The first announcement of the government order was widely publicized and stressed the penalties for failure to comply, which at the time were drastic, with stiff jail sentences. The order accomplished what it intended and millions of dollars in gold coin were deposited in banks and Federal Reserves.

It is regrettable that, because of the hysteria of the time, many really rare gold coins were turned in. The government was not interested in the coins themselves, but only in hoards. Within a few weeks the original order, which exempted gold coins in quantities of $100 was amended to exempt gold coins that were considered rare and held in coin collections. Over a period of years subsequent amendments gradually continued to ease the stringency of the original order. At first limits were lifted with the exception of two-and-one-half-dollar pieces. Restrictions on the two-and-one-half-dollar pieces limited ownership to not more than two of any date or mint mark. This restriction was lifted next and the offense was changed from a criminal to a civil one with a fine.

Since the Hoarding Act of 1933, interest in gold coin collecting has been growing by leaps and bounds. As soon as the government discontinued making gold coins, collectors began taking great interest in them.

There are no restrictions regarding the export or import, purchase, sale, or collecting of gold coins in the United States of any date.

4.

PRIVATE

GOLD COINS

Necessity has brought into reality many things, and so, through a necessity, we have our private territorial gold coins. These pieces were issued between 1830 and 1862 in different parts of our country to answer a demand for denominations lacking in regular issues. While there were laws that forbade the individual states striking gold coins, there were none forbidding private persons or private companies doing so.

In 1787, the year before Washington was elected to the presidency, a jeweler named Ephraim Brasher, whose place of business was on Cherry Street in New York City, appealed to the state legislature for permission to strike copper coins to circulate in that state. Permission was refused, but that did not stop him from using the dies he had made. He struck his coins in gold, their intrinsic value being $16, the same as the Spanish doubloons. They were known as the Ephraim Brasher doubloons. The one with EB on the right wing of the eagle is one of the highest priced coins in the world.

The years 1830–40 saw great industrial development and territorial expansion in our country. The first steam locomotive, streetcar, and omnibus were put to use; the Erie Canal was built and the telegraph invented.

In 1830, a treaty with Great Britain opened to American commerce the ports of the West Indies and South America; a treaty with Turkey opened the Black Sea. Around the same time, Templeton Reid, assayer, located near the gold mines in Lumpkin County, Georgia, issued the first of his private gold coins. It is not definitely known just how long his business existed or just when it started, but the first coins to bear his stamp were dated 1830. The coins issued from his Georgia establishment contained gold of a higher standard and fineness than any other ever issued by either private persons or the government. It is reasonable to assume that this is why so many were melted, resulting in their great scarcity.

Christopher Bechtler's establishment was located in Rutherford County, North Carolina. The first of his coins, although undated, are attributed to the early part of 1831. About 1842, he passed his business on to his son August, who continued until about 1852. The gold for these pieces came from North Carolina and Georgia.

When Texas was admitted to the Union as an independent state, arbitration over the boundary resulted in the war with Mexico and ended with the Treaty of Guadeloupe in 1848. For $18,000,000 Mexico sold all of her northern territory to the United States. This territory included the region known as California, Utah, Nevada, New Mexico, and part of Colorado and Arizona.

Civilization had already pushed its way westward when the cry of "gold" came from California and resounded from coast to coast. There was a great exodus from the east; people poured into the west in droves. The trials and hardships of the cross-country trek with inadequate means did not stop them. With the influx of prospectors, traders, merchants, and people from every walk of life, towns grew up overnight. It was the dawn of a Golden Age. The forty-niner was staking his claim.

The discovery of gold in California was a boon to a world suffering from a gold shortage. It changed the whole outlook of industry and commerce. Prices skyrocketed to unbelievable heights. For a while gold dust was used as a medium of exchange, but this was soon found to be cumbersome and impractical. The demand for gold coins was great but there were no mints in the west. To ship gold dust to the east to be minted into coins was out of the question. Besides not having adequate means for shipping, there were the hazards of holdups, Indians, and slow progress overland. An attempt was made by the provincial government in the Oregon Territory to establish a mint, but this failed. A private organization, the Oregon Exchange Company, started operations in Oregon City in 1849. They employed a blacksmith to make the apparatus and an engraver, who happened to be one of the company's members, to make the dies.

The Mormons, who for years had been migrating westward, having been expelled from New York, Illinois, and Nebraska, finally settled on the shores of the Great Salt Lake in Utah, while it was still Mexican territory. They started their mint in 1849, striking coins from the gold dust received from California. Their twenty-dollar gold piece was the first to be struck in this country, but the intrinsic value was found to be only between $16 and $18.

There were about fifteen private mints operating in California between 1849 and 1855, striking millions of dollars worth of gold coins. Norris, Greig & Norris coined the first, a five-dollar coin of 1849; Moffat & Company struck the first ten-dollar coin; Baldwin & Company, the first twenty; Moffat & Company, the first fifty. The fifty-dollar coin was octagonal, bearing the stamp of the United States Assayer Augustus Humbert. F.D. Kohler & Company and Moffat & Company issued ingots stamped from gold bars. The last private issue coins from California came from the mints of Wass, Mollitar & Company and Kellogg & Company, dated 1855, just one year after the San Francisco Mint was opened.

In 1857 a panic overtook the country due to over-capitalization, over-building of railroads, rise of prices, speculation, bad crops, bad state banking, and diminishing gold output. While there was agitation between the states over the question of states' rights and the Dred Scott Decision, the first Atlantic cable was being laid. Silver was discovered in Nevada and a new gold district was discovered in the west. The forty-niner rush was repeated but not in the same proportions as the rush a decade before; the states' rebellion had become a serious issue.

There were three private minting firms in Colorado. The first coins to be struck were by Clark, Gruber & Company, in 1860. Coins of all United States gold denominations with the exception of ones and threes were issued. In 1862, the government purchased the Clark, Gruber establishment, which was thereafter conducted as a United States Assay Office. The original bill called for a government mint at Denver, but this did not materialize until 1906.

John Parsons & Company, Tarryall Mines, and J.J. Conway & Company, Georgia Gulch, operated their private mints at about the same time for a limited period. Parsons issued quarter eagles and half eagles; Conway, quarter eagles, half eagles, and eagles. None of the coins bore dates, but they are said to have been struck in 1861. All are quite rare, Conway's exceedingly so.

The designs on these privately issued gold coins are varied. Some are very plain with only the name of the mint or minter, date, and denomination or weight. Others have very attractive original designs, and still others are so very much like the regular government coinage that to the ordinary layman they are easily mistaken.

5.

THE COINS
OF THE MORMONS

"During the year 1846, the beginning of the great exodus from Nauvoo, Illinois, to Salt Lake Valley, Utah, there appeared a strange little brass token that has created and attracted the attention of church members and collectors from all over the country" (*Numismatist*, July, 1911, p. 241). The date and Brigham Young's favorite emblem—the beehive, meaning "Let everyone do his duty," and clasped hands, signifying friendship—indicate very strongly that the coin is associated with the Mormons. However, some believe that it is in no way connected with the Mormons, because the emblem of the beehive was first thought of after their arrival in the valley. We do not know whether this token was used as an exchange medium or as a commemorative issue, nor do we know what its value was. Its size was about that of a dime.

When the Mormons went west, they took very little money with them and droughts, insects, and other adverse conditions drained what money they had. Hard work ultimately conquered all their handicaps and eventually Indians were no longer a threat. Trade and barter were their mediums of exchange. A Mormon battalion in the Mexican War brought home with them, in 1847, a certain amount of money which circulated. It is recorded that Captain James Brown left the valley in 1847 to collect his men's back pay, returning with $5,000 in Spanish gold doubloons valued at $16 each. Many other instances of small quantities of coin coming into the hands of the Mormons are on record, but the discovery of gold in the ground was the start of a desire to issue coins.

A very interesting and integral part of the Mormons' history was contributed by Thomas Rhoads, more commonly referred to as Father Rhoads. Rhoads and his family left Missouri in the spring of 1846 for Sutter's Fort on the Sacramento River. Upon arriving at the fort, Rhoads and his five sons signed up for service in the Mexican War. After termination of their services they returned to Sutter's Fort just in time to help organize a party for the purpose of rescuing a snowbound Donner party trapped in the California mountains. The small rescue party was successful in its attempt to locate the lost Donner party, but unfortunately did not arrive in time to save the group from starvation. Only a few members of the Donner party survived.

On their way home, hunger once again reared its ugly head, for the bears had eaten the supplies that members of the rescue party had tied to the trees to aid them on their return trip. The party finally reached civilization once again, but not before scarcity of food compelled them to eat the rawhides from their snowshoes.

When gold was discovered in the channel of the mill race at Sutter's Sawmill, Rhoads and his sons joined the other adventurers in their quest for gold, which later proved very rewarding. After accumulating a small fortune, Rhoads and his family left

California for Great Salt Lake in the latter part of 1848. News of the Rhoads fortune leaked out and while they were making their way through the California mountains they were attacked by bandits. Had it not been for the intervention of some passing travelers, the ambush might have been successful. With the help of the travelers, the Rhoads family was able to repel the attack.

According to Colonel Lock, Father Rhoads brought with him several sacks of gold, among which there was a 60-pound sack, the largest amount that had been brought into the valley. Father Rhoads turned all the gold over to Brigham Young, who in return had a home built for Rhoads and allowed him to withdraw from the tithing office all the food supplies that he deemed necessary. Rhoads also received a herd of cattle in consideration for the gold dust. It was customary for each individual to give one-tenth of his accomplishments to the church, whether cattle, produce, or money, in order to aid their common cause. But Father Rhoads contributed his entire amount in order to accelerate the progress of the Mormon people. The famous 60-pound sack of gold was the chief topic of the people in the valley at that time and for quite some time to come.

Concerning gold dust that was brought into the valley, William T. Fullett, a battalion member, was credited with having made the first deposit on December 10, 1848. He deposited fourteen and one-half ounces of gold dust which was then worth $232, equal to $16 per ounce. Within four months, close to $8,000 in dust and a little coin was deposited in the "bank." Entries of deposit show that battalion men deposited 77 percent, and 135 others, 35 percent of the total.

Since the city was fairly well supplied with gold dust, the council unanimously agreed that it was time to convert the dust into coins. In order to accomplish this, President Young solicited the aid of John Kay and John Taylor in planning the first mint ever to be established in the Great Salt Lake Valley.

John Kay, skilled in patternmaking, and John Taylor were persuaded to work on suitable designs for the coins. After some time and difficulty, the preparations were finally completed and Kay began to melt the gold and roll it into sheets. A punching press was then used in punching out the gold discs, while a coining press stamped the designs on the discs.

Kay turned out ten-dollar pieces which were paid out at a premium of fifty cents on the piece. Whether the coins were at a premium because of the novelty value or because of overweight is not known. Twenty of them were charged out to Brigham Young and five to John Kay. A week later twenty-one pieces were coined and charged out at par to Brigham Young. No more were coined until September, 1849, because the crucibles were broken in the preliminary runs and melting could not be continued until others were obtained.

Since the coining could not be continued, the punching press was dismantled and shipped by ox team to Parowan where it could be put to use while the crucibles were being made. During the short time the press was in Parowan, it was used for cutting nails. The sheet iron was cut into strips and then headed in a vise. On October, 1848, the press was returned to the valley where it was used in connection with the coinage of the 1849–50 gold coins and later, the 1860 gold coins.

Finally, the patternmaker Kay completed his work on refining the gold dust, and at last the mint was ready for operation. In order to test the crucibles, Kay struck a few pattern pieces bearing a design on only one side. This time the crucibles did not break. Apparently the workers were satisfied with the results, because the mint went into full production and remained so for the remainder of the year.

Joseph Fielding Smith, church historian, made the following statement concerning the men who participated in the coining of these gold coins:

> When the Desert Mint was built, Alfred B. Lambson forged all the dies and punches, in fact all that pertained to the mint with the exception of the drop hammer, which was forged by Martin H. Beck. John Kay cut the dies and coined the money, William Clayton and Thomas Bullock being associated with him as accountant and weigher. As an expedient, before this Dr. Willard Richards weighed the gold dust brought from California and placed it in small packages, representing from $1 to $20 which passed current for money.[1]

---

[1] By permission of the Church Historian, Church of Jesus Christ of Latter-Day Saints; reprinted from *Mormon Money* by Sheridan L. McGarry.

The designs on the pieces were not too elaborate, but one must admit originality and much praise should be forthcoming for the job they did with such limited facilities.

The following is a description of the gold coins minted in Salt Lake City: on the obverse in the center, there are clasped hands with the date 1849 below; the legend reads "G.S.L.C.P.G." (Great Salt Lake City Pure Gold), "Two and half Do." On the reverse is a crown over the all-seeing eye, around the edge of which are the words "HOLINESS TO THE LORD." The designs on the 1849 and 1859 coins were all the same with the exception of the 1850 five-dollar piece. This had nine stars around the edge and a slightly different crown.

It is generally believed that during the early coinage no effort was made to assay or refine the gold because there was no one connected with the mint capable of determining such standards. This fact has been substantiated by Captain H. Stansbury in his report on his exploration and survey of the Great Salt Lake. The coinage was done in good faith, however, because of the then prevailing theory of "relative fineness"; in other words, the Mormons based the worth of all gold upon the purity of California gold. Little did they realize that the coins minted from native gold were very low in assay due to the fineness of the gold, although it was full weight. According to Colonel Lock, the 1849 five-dollar gold piece was actually worth $4.51. This mistake was later brought to light but not before losses had been sustained by many who had purchased gold on the relative-fineness theory.

6.

CIVIL WAR

MONEY

Southern guns roared on Fort Sumter and the Civil War had begun. Our nation had started the bloodiest war in its history.

Patriotism ran high in the newly formed Confederacy, and the cry went out for all to help in the war effort by turning in their gold, silver, and other precious metals in exchange for both state and Confederate notes. Southern bonds were issued to finance the war—all with promises to pay a certain number of years after the ratification of peace between the North and South. There was no question about who would win—the South of course! And this temporary paper money was just as good as having the gold coins it represented—or so they thought.

Financing the war was no easy task. The South, not having much heavy industry of its own, had to rely on foreign aid for its sorely needed supplies—which it had to pay for with hard cash.

Coins soon went out of circulation. There was an attempt to continue operation of the New Orleans mint, but, due to lack of metal, this failed, and the only coins that were struck there for the Confederacy were the cent and half-dollar—both experimental pieces, and very rare. The Dahlonaga and Charlotte mints were closed for good.

As the war progressed and things began looking blacker, public confidence waned. There was a scramble for gold, and some state bank notes (formerly considered "as good as gold") were redeemed for gold at "20 cents on the dollar."

As more and more money was needed, more and more Confederate paper was printed. Great quantities were printed in 1864—the last year this paper money was issued. Printing presses were turning out denominations anywhere from fifty-cent notes up to five-hundred-dollar bills.

The collapse of the Southern effort put an end to this, and rendered all Confederate money valueless; the land was left destitute as a result. While much of the money was destroyed, some found its way into attics, in cartons and trunks, where it lay for decades—a useless reminder of the great war effort. Many stories have been told since of old Southern families with trunks full of Confederate money stored in their attics.

The vastly increased interest in numismatics over the past two decades has brought much of this currency out of its storage places. There are a few rarities in existence, such as the Montgomery, Alabama $1,000 and $500 notes, plus a few others, which are worth more today than their original face value. The majority, however, are worth less.

The start of the war in the North was quite different, however. Heavily industrialized, the North was far better equipped to cope with the problems presented by the war.

There too, small change soon went out of circulation. The loss of the New Orleans mint cut coin output in half, throwing the burden of coin manufacture on the shoulders of the Philadelphia and San Francisco mints. Although these mints were also hampered by the shortage of metal, they were not nearly as hard hit as the South.

Contributing to the great shortage of hard cash was the desire of many to hoard and the greatly increased need for small change in day-to-day business transactions. Housewives going to market were constantly plagued by a lack of change; merchants, therefore, were compelled to improvise methods of providing change, with the result that postage stamps were frequently used for this purpose. While a necessity, the use of stamps for this purpose was a nuisance since the stamps often stuck together, lost their gum (one reason why so many of our early issues are found in mint condition without gum), and were very fragile.

A year after the war began, a Mr. J. Gault patented the first encased postage stamps. This consisted of a round brassy metal frame in which stamps of various denominations were inserted and covered with a transparent mica cover. It protected the stamp, served the purpose of a coin and could be used much longer because of its cover. Denominations issued were for one, two, three, five, ten, twelve, twenty-four, thirty, and ninety cents.

The enterprising Mr. Gault arranged to have advertising placed on the back cover, and while many have his name on them, dozens of Northern firms paid to use this convenient method of providing change. Outstanding among these are such concerns as Ayers Pills, Drakes Plantation Bitters, Burnetts Cooking Extracts, Lord and Taylor, North American Insurance Co., etc. All of these encased postage stamps are quite rare—the highest-valued ones being those stamps in the higher denominations.

Another answer to the coin shortage was the series known as Civil War Tokens. They first appeared the latter part of 1861, and were coined in great quantities until 1864, when laws—still in effect today—abolished all *private* money coining. It is estimated that about fifty million of these tokens were coined during this period, in two main varieties: patriotic ones, with novel political legends—"our flag, should anyone tear it down, shoot him on the spot"; "millions for contractors, not one cent for widows", etc., and merchants' tokens, which appeared with legends advertising wares. Although these were not legitimate money, they were used as cents.

The war had caused the suspension of specie payments, and all coins had gone out of circulation; hoarding was universal. Copper-nickel cents of 1859–64 were worth a premium.

The situation was serious, something had to be done. In 1862, Congress passed a bill authorizing postage currency. Notes in denominations of 5c., 10c., 25c., and 50c., had facsimiles of the current 5c. and 10c. postage stamps printed on them. This was brought about by the wide use of postage stamps as small change. While not favored, the system was used.

In 1863, a new act was passed authorizing the first issue of Fractional Currency. This currency circulated until as late as 1876, when an act authorized its redemption in silver coin.

During 1866 and 1867, the Treasury Department made up special Fractional Currency shields. These were an ornate arrangement of specimen notes, printed on one side and framed. They included notes of all issues, both obverse and reverse, for the first three series. The 15c. Grant and Sherman notes were included, even though these never appeared in circulation. Shields were distributed to banks to assist them in detecting counterfeits. These shields are quite rare and difficult to find in good condition. Many were taken apart in the hope that the notes could be sold or spent.

Before the Civil War, State Bank charters were easy to obtain. The rapid expansion of our economy had created the need for more money and State Banks were authorized to issue paper money against their deposits. This system was satisfactory as long as there was prosperity; in recession, however, deposits were withdrawn, banks closed their doors, and money became valueless.

While paper money was looked upon with suspicion, the government was compelled to issue its first currency: the demand notes of 1861 and the legal tender notes of 1862 and 1863. Issued in denominations of from one dollar to one thousand dollars, they were called "greenbacks" from the color on the reverse side.

The one-dollar and two-dollar denominations were often sent to the "boys in blue" at the front. It became the practice to pin these notes to a heavy piece of paper so they could not be detected in the mails, and stolen. Many of the notes of this series we find today have these pin holes in them.

With the termination of hostilities, changes in minting procedures came about. In the South, the mint in New Orleans was not permitted to resume operations until 1879, and for over a decade it only issued silver dollars. In the West, a new mint was opened in 1870 at Carson City. The San Francisco mint continued to operate, turning out gold coins. The Philadelphia mint bore the brunt of our nation's small-change needs. As the economy gradually got back on a normal footing, change was again available in our pockets.

7.

HARD TIMES

TOKENS

During the stirring period from 1832 to 1844, politics and the economy of the country produced the Hard Times Tokens.

President Andrew Jackson disapproved of a fiscal system under which public funds were deposited in a single, privately controlled institution—the Bank of the United States. In 1832 Jackson vetoed the bill to continue the Bank's existence after the expiration of its charter in 1836. This was in opposition to Clay and the financial interests of the country. This caused an upheaval in both political parties.

Jackson's party split into two opposed groups. And Clay's supporters fought to restore the bank. Jackson and his successor, Martin Van Buren, succeeded in warding off the attacks and put in reforms.

They discontinued depositing funds in the Bank of the United States and established a Sub-Treasury system. Metallic currency was the only medium of payment for public lands.

At the time the country was undergoing a severe depression. That, plus the uncertainty of the banking system, led to hoarding hard money. Paper money was so unreliable, nobody wanted to accept it. The demand on the large cent, and the disappearance of small change, led to the manufacture of the Hard Times Tokens. Those with political slogans were the first campaign tokens.

Some of the legends on the Political Tokens are as follows:

"Andrew Jackson President Elected 1828 re-elected 1832—We commemorate the glorious victories of our hero in war and in peace."

"Gulian C. Verplanck Our Next Govnr A Faithful friend of our Country."

Small bust of Jackson with "My Substitute for the U.S. Bank. My Experiment, My Currency, My Glory." A running boar: "My Victory, My third Heat, Down with the Bank, Perish Credit, Perish Commerce."

Running Jackass: "I follow in the steps of my illustrious predecessor." Turtle with strongbox on its back marked "Sub Treasury." "Executive Experiment."

Balking horse: "Constitution as I understand it," "Roman Firmness," "A Plain System Void of Pomp."

Jackson sitting in a strongbox with a sword and a bag of money: "I take the responsibility." Sailing vessel named "Constitution" wrecked: "Van Buren Metallic Currency."

Phoenix: "Substitute for shin-plasters," "Specie payments suspended May 10, 1837" in wreath.

Ship "Constitution" under full sail: "Webster credit Currency." Ship named "Experiment" wrecked on the rocks: "Van Buren Metallic Currency."

Slave tokens: "Am I Not a Man and Brother." Another: "Am I not a Woman and Sister."

There are many varieties of "Liberty Heads" similar to large United States cents. Some are very ugly. In addition to some of the reverses already mentioned they are also found with "Millions for Defense, Not One Cent for Tribute"; "Mint Drop Bentonian Currency"; "Mint Drop Benton Experiment"; Ugly Head obverse with "Loco Foco" instead of "Liberty" on headband.

Many enterprising merchants of the day issued tokens advertising their wares to be used as small change. Some of these tokens have the same obverses as the Political Tokens.

Others have the type of business on them—a clock-maker has a clock; a boot-maker, a boot; a barber, a comb and scissors. A gold-beater has an arm and sledge, an anvil represents hardware and cutlery. A circus rider on two horses stands for the Hippodrome, and a railroad coach for the New York and Harlem Railroad.

Edwin Parmele's liquor store has an inebriate with a glass. An agriculturist has a bull. An umbrella-maker has an open umbrella, and a chair-maker, an upright chair. Public baths are indicated by a nude.

Lyman H. Low listed 183 Hard Times and Merchants' Tokens from 1832 to 1844. While many are easily available, there are others which are rare.

They were made in bronze, brass, and white metal, the bronze being the commonest. The majority were made the size of large cents but there are a few of smaller.

8.

COMMEMORATIVE
COINS

The opening of the Chicago World's Fair in 1892 was the occasion for the issue of our first commemorative coins, the Columbian half dollars. Designed to help defray expenses, they did not at first meet with great enthusiasm. A good many were coined in 1892 and still more in 1893. It was hoped that nearly 2,500,000 of both dates could be sold at one dollar each.

Many were sold, brought home by visitors, and kept for years as souvenirs of the exposition. A great many, however, did not sell and ultimately were placed in circulation at face value. For many years it was not unusual to receive one of these Columbian half dollars, particularly one dated 1893, in one's pocket change. The Isabella quarters, struck in 1893, were issued in much smaller quantities and therefore were not a drug on the market as the Columbian halves were.

Even though these commemoratives did not meet with great enthusiasm, the series was started, as if by accident, and the idea of selling special coins at premiums to raise money for special events took hold.

In 1900 we had our first and only commemorative dollar, the Washington Lafayette. Until this time no special denomination had been adopted for commemorative coins and they began to appear in all kinds. With the advent of the 1903 Louisiana Purchase commemorative gold dollars, we have the first of a series of gold dollars and quarter eagles. The Panama-Pacific fifty-dollar slugs, which appeared in 1915 became very rare. Coined in very limited numbers they were issued more as historical souvenirs than as coins. Even so, at the time of issue, trouble was encountered disposing of them at over face value.

People resented having to pay a premium for a coin, no matter how interesting it was or how small an issue. Little did those buyers know how greatly they would increase in value. Even in the late 1920s, dealers were more than pleased to get their capital investment out of the Panama-Pacific fifty-dollar piece plus a small premium for their efforts. I can remember the pair, both octagonal and round, being offered, uncirculated, for as little as $125 for the pair! Twenty-five dollars over face value!

While approximately a thousand of these Panama-Pacific fifty-dollar pieces were struck of each type, nearly half of them were turned in to the mint to be melted up. This leaves a little over a thousand of both in existence today.

The Panama-Pacific set—the two fifty-dollar gold pieces, a gold quarter eagle, a gold dollar, and a fifty-cent piece—created the first great urge to encourage more of this interesting series. This commemoration, having adopted so many different denominations, helped decide what future denomination was to be used—the half dollar. Since both the price and the size of the half dollar were the most popular, future commemorative coins were struck in this denomination, soon exclusively. In 1918 the Lincoln Centennial half dollar was issued, and from 1920 on, one or more different commemoratives came out every year.

Difficulty was found selling all the commemoratives that were authorized, for while the series had enlisted many ardent followers, there were not as many as there were coins. Many were available and kept the values down for a long while. Collectors were told these commemoratives were limited issues and would become valuable, but did not respond.

In 1921, the idea of making varieties that would be rarer than the regular series was first put into effect. We find the Missouri Centennial with and without star and the Grant Memorial with and without star and the two Alabamas. This was the first step toward trying to sell more coins to a limited number of buyers. As time went by, many commemorative halves were issued, some by associations which only wanted to dispose of enough coins to fill their need for funds. More enterprising concerns had the halves made for many years, from many mints, and with all kinds of minor varieties to create rarities.

The quantity of commemorative coins issued hit its peak around 1935–36. Interest at that time also hit a peak. Speculators and collectors were getting on the band wagon, buying commemoratives in quantities, making up sets, and carrying around graphs showing the fluctuations of price trends. It was not unusual for "the boys" to deal in hundreds and thousands of one issue. It was similar to stock market speculation. Some rare issues skyrocketed from $5 to $75 within a week! Such rapid profits were unheard of in the numismatic world.

As might have been expected, it couldn't last. The crash came. Overnight no one wanted to buy any commemoratives and everyone was loaded with hundreds of one kind. It took many years to get over this debacle and for holders of commemoratives to dispose of their hoards. When this finally occurred, most issues were widely distributed, and a gradual and more secure rise in values began.

The sale of new issues after 1936 was very difficult, and the government approved few. For many years the only new commemoratives struck were those under authorization from previous years, such as the Boone, Oregon Trail, Texas, and Arkansas. Very few coins were struck each year because of the sharply reduced demand and the repetition of designs. Collectors were disgusted with the "rackets" as they called them. Some hope was raised with the issue of the 1946 Iowa Centennial, for this was a new, single, and interesting coin. However, it was quickly followed by the mass of varieties of the Booker T. Washington and Washington-Carver series, the last of which, with thirty different varieties, ended in 1954.

At present the administration, on the advice of the Mint, frowns upon commemorative issues. The exploitation of many issues of the series has caused a good deal of discontent. The feeling is that the Mint is too busy to issue these special coins and that commemoratives tend to confuse the coinage of the country, creating too many designs. It is also felt that commemoratives should be issued in the form of medals. Medals, however, have never reached the popularity among collectors that coins have; the collector likes to feel his collection is of basic intrinsic value, no matter how small. The number of medals versus proof sets issued by the Mint is evidence of this.

It is too bad the situation has come to such an impasse. I feel a series of commemorative coins is educational, interesting, and can within reason be a profitable investment. The fault lies in the manner of distribution.

9.

TEDDY ROOSEVELT'S
TWENTY-DOLLAR GOLD PIECE

The Smithsonian Institution received the donation by Cornelius Roosevelt, of Washington, D.C., of an experimental high-relief double eagle or twenty-dollar gold piece, dated 1907, designed by Augustus St. Gaudens at the request of President Theodore Roosevelt. This is one of the great rarities of the United States coin series and has, in addition, an unusual historical connotation since it was owned originally by Theodore Roosevelt, who devoted considerable efforts toward its design and production.

In fact, in the winter of 1905, Theodore Roosevelt met at a dinner in Washington with Augustus St. Gaudens, whose sculptures the president admired greatly. The conversation drifted to the beauty of ancient Greek coins, described by St. Gaudens as almost the only coins of real artistic merit. Why couldn't the United States have coins as beautiful as the Greek ones, the president wished to know. If St. Gaudens would model them, the president said, he would have them minted.

Thus started a unique venture in modern monetary history. Manifesting his versatility and extraordinary energy, Theodore Roosevelt found the time personally to conduct the campaign for a more artistic series of United States coinage designs. On November 6, 1905, in a letter to St. Gaudens regarding these designs, the president said:

> I want to make a suggestion. It seems to me worthwhile to try for a really good coinage; though I suppose there will be a revolt about it! I was looking at some gold coins of Alexander the Great today, and I was struck by their high relief. Would it not be well to have our coins in high relief, and also to have the rims raised? The point of having the rims raised would be, of course, to protect the figure on the coin; and if we have the figures in high relief, like the figures on the old Greek coins, they will surely last longer. What do you think of this?

For two years president and sculptor gave much time and energy to the task of producing the new coin designs. The models finally adopted for the double eagle were of unusual artistic merit. The obverse showed a standing figure of "Liberty," holding aloft in her right hand the torch of enlightenment and in her left, the olive branch of peace. On the reverse side was a rendering of a flying eagle above a rising sun.

A few experimental pieces having an extremely high relief were struck at the president's order. These exceedingly rare pieces can be easily distinguished from the ones issued later for general circulation, which also have a very high relief. The field of the rare experimental pieces is excessively concave and connects directly with the edge without any border, giving it a sharp knifelike appearance. Liberty's skirt shows two folds on the side of the right leg; the Capitol building in the background at the left is very small; and the date, 1907, is in Roman numerals. The sun, on the reverse side, has fourteen rays.

In addition to these experimental pieces, 11,250 high-relief twenty-dollar gold pieces were struck on a medal press for general distribution and may be found today in many collections. Their relief is somewhat lower than that of the experimental pieces. They have a border around the edge; Liberty's skirt has three folds on the side of the right leg; the Capitol is considerably larger; and the date, 1907, is indicated in Roman numerals. On the reverse, there are only thirteen rays extending from the sun.

For practical reasons and especially since these high-relief coins could not be struck on a regular coin press and would not stack, it was decided soon to revert to the customary flat relief. A large number of similar flat-relief double eagles were issued in 1907 (these pieces show the date in Arabic numerals) and in later years up to 1933, when the issuance of gold coins was discontinued.

Theodore Roosevelt's twenty-dollar gold piece, donated by Cornelius Roosevelt, is placed on permanent display in the Smithsonian Institution's hall of monetary history. It should remind us of Roosevelt's words about this piece: "Certain things were done, of which the economic bearing was more remote but which bore directly upon our welfare, because they add to the beauty of living and therefore to the joy of life."

10.

AMERICA'S FIRST
COLONIAL COINS

The first New England coins, crude silver pieces with a simple
design "NE" on the obverse, "XII" on the reverse, were the first
coins struck in the Colonies. Shortage of change and the
inability to get relief from the mother country prompted the
Massachusetts Colony to embark upon this coining adventure to
alleviate this shortage in New England. The famous Pine Tree
Shilling shown below was part of this series to be struck by John
Hull, who was appointed Mint Master.

After several years, when the coining operations were brought
to the attention of King Charles of England, action was taken to
prohibit any further issues.

While the majority were dated 1652, it is thought that they
were coined for thirty years despite the King's disapproval.
These crude and early pieces are actively sought by collectors
and bring good prices today. They were coined in shillings,
sixpence, three-pence and two-penny pieces.

11.
CHRISTIAN GOBRECHT'S
FLYING EAGLE DOLLAR

In the year 1836 interest was revived in the coining of silver dollars, as none had been coined since 1803. With the proposed passage of a law reducing their weight, permission was granted to resume minting this denomination.

Christian Gobrecht, famed engraver, executed the dies for this beautiful coin shown here. The Liberty Seated design was submitted by Thomas Sully, famed Philadelphia artist, and the Flying Eagle on the reverse was designed by Titian Peale, son of Charles Willson Peale, famous painter.

In 1836, 1838 and 1839 limited quantities of these dollars were struck with minor varieties on a more or less experimental basis. All are very rare.

It was not until 1840 that the dollar came into its own. Robert Ball Hughes, an Anglo-American sculptor, was the designer. He closely copied the Liberty Seated design on the obverse, but changed the Eagle to a standing position on the reverse. This famous Liberty Seated design was used on dollars and smaller denominations from then until 1891.

12.

HISTORY

OF THE "DOLLAR"

From the time of the Roman Empire, and through the Dark Ages the predominant size of silver coins was copied after the Ancient Roman Denarius, about the size of our present day dime. Times were pretty lean and silver pieces were consequently few and far between.

In the year 1516 a rich silver mine was discovered in Joachim's dale, a mining district in Bohemia. The count of Schlitz, by whom it was appropriated, struck a great number of large silver coins. The first had the date 1518 and the effigy of St. Joachim upon it. These were to be of the same value in silver as the many gold *gulden* then in use in trade. This Joachimsthaler has the distinction of being known as the first "Thaler" or silver coin of approximately one ounce in weight and around the size of our silver dollars.

From that time on the "thaler" became one of the most popular coins in Europe. Most countries and German states issued hundreds of varieties of these. The French issued coins of similar size "Ecus", the English their "Crowns", the Spanish their "Pieces of 8" (8 Reals). The name of such coins in other countries were changed to "Daler", "Dalar", "Daalder", "Tallero".

In the Western Hemisphere the Spanish "Pieces of 8" circulated widely during Colonial days. The British kept as much English Specie as possible from the American Colonies, creating serious shortages here. They also prohibited the coinage of coins. It is therefore not surprising the Spanish 8 Real coins soon became the principal medium to circulate and soon became known as the "Spanish Milled Dollar".

It is said that the Dollar George Washington threw across the Rapahannock River was one of these and indeed it must have been for our country did not coin any silver dollars until 1794.

We sometimes wonder why we did not adopt the English Denominations when we first started coining. Pounds, shillings and pence were used in all transactions with England, the parent country, during the Colonial days. We find that early Colonial paper money was issued in English denominations but during and after the Revolution one finds the gradual change to dollars and cents, some of the earlier notes even being redeemable in "Spanish Milled Dollars". No doubt antagonism over the war with England and the use of the Spanish coins influenced our country to adopt the dollar and cents denominations.

Our silver dollar has had a stormy path. From 1794 through 1803 they were coined in varying quantities. From 1803 through 1840 we have a gap of thirty-seven years when none were coined for circulation. It seems the amount of silver contained in the early dollars was too great. In 1837 Congress passed a law providing that 3½ grains of the alloy be extracted from the authorized weight of the dollar which at that time weighed 416 grains. This made the new dollar weight 412½ grains. The only dollars struck between 1803 and 1840 were the 1804s of questionable authenticity, and the rare pattern or experimental pieces of 1836, 1838 and 1839, forerunners of the regular issued Liberty Seated dollars of 1840.

Standard silver dollars were again suspended with the issue of Trade dollars in 1873, designed to capture trade in the Orient. As these were not successful they were terminated in 1878 and standard silver dollars were again coined from then on until 1904. The few Trade dollars that were issued between 1879 and 1885 were struck for collectors only. In 1904 all dollars were discontinued due to the lack of bullion.

The Peace dollar first made its appearance in 1921, seventeen years later, and was coined continuously from then until 1935, the last year silver dollars were struck.

13.
OUR
FIRST GOLD COINS

The half eagle, or five dollar gold piece, was the first gold coin struck by our mint in accordance with the Coining Act of April 1792. Dated 1795, it had liberty's head facing right with a turban-like headdress. The reverse shows an eagle with spread wings, holding a wreath of laurel in its beak and standing on a palm branch. The original of this design was thought to be copied from a Roman first century B. C. onyx cameo, of similar design.

In addition to half eagles, limited quantities of quarter eagles and eagles were coined, but only on demand. Half eagles were our mint's major output. Even so, these were issued in very limited quantities.

The revaluation of our gold coins in 1834 is felt responsible for the extreme rarity of our early pieces. It is thought many were returned to the mint to be melted in order to get the benefit of the new values. For each $100 worth of old type coins, one could get at least $106.

Reverse designs were changed in 1797 to a spread eagle shown above. It was not until 1807 with the second design change that denominations were placed upon our gold.

14.

HOW TO DETERMINE WHETHER
A COIN IS UNCIRCULATED

I cannot stress enough the importance of accurate classification on condition in coins. If one becomes a coin collector, this exacting work should be the first to be mastered. A good amount of money can be lost by paying high prices for coins or coin collections that have been grossly overrated. If, when buying coins, there is any doubt in your mind as to whether a certain piece is in the condition represented, take it to an expert or another experienced collector. He will gladly give you an opinion free of charge. When purchasing a large collection, don't hesitate to have a dealer appraise it for you and give you his written expert opinion. It may cost you a fee for an expert appraisal, but this sum may save you many hundreds in the long run. Dealers KNOW what to look for.

With the steadily increasing values of uncirculated coins, it is essential that the serious collector know how to determine whether or not a coin is really uncirculated. Because of some of the cleaning processes used today, very careful scrutiny is necessary. I do not mean a cleaned coin cannot be considered uncirculated; what I mean is that many cleaned coins look like uncirculated pieces when closer scrutiny shows they have some wear.

It must be remembered that truly uncirculated pieces, if properly cleaned, are not decreased in value, even though under some circumstances it is preferable to have uncirculated pieces in their natural state. Too frequently, we look at a coin and, because it appears bright and new, consider it uncirculated, when the actual wear upon such a piece should be the determining factor.

I shall try to describe what I have found to be the first spots to wear on a coin, the first places to look for wear on what appears to be an uncirculated coin. I shall also mention other telltale defects to watch for.

Lincoln cents show their first wear on the cheekbone of Lincoln's bust. In the twenties, for a few years, Lincoln cents were struck very poorly so the coinage appears blurred, and these would be exceptions to the rule. Such blurred coins, even though uncirculated, would not be considered choice uncirculated coins.

Indian Heads first show wear on the obverse at the lock of hair at the lower right-hand bottom part of the bust. The ribbon hanging down is next to show wear. On the reverse, the highlights of the bow at the bottom of the wreath first wear.

The tip of the headdress above the word "Liberty" first shows wear on a large cent back to 1840. Prior to that date, the hairlock below the headdress, the eyebrow, and the cheek give telltale evidence. On the reverse, the highlighted leaves in the wreaths must be watched for wear. These coins are rather well struck. They should also be watched for minute scratches on the field of the obverse and reverse, on the head, and most important of all, on the edges of the coin. I have seen large cents that appear to have no wear at all, but close examination shows they contain many tiny scratches and nicks which immediately remove them from the uncirculated category.

Color plays a vitally important part in the valuation of large cents. Rich browns and steel color are the most desirable. Partially red, red, and brilliant are less desirable because they are apt to corrode under certain conditions.

The earlier large cents are a study for an expert. Being crudely struck and with so many varieties, it is difficult to name any specific places of where to look for wear. Each coin must be examined with the greatest care. Look for minute tiny scratches. Examine the color of the coin and its glossy surface. Should one of these "seem" to be worn slightly, it might well be the manner in which it was struck.

The most desirable condition for an early large cent is one with a rich dark brown, glossy surface, well centered, evenly struck, with no apparent signs of wear, corrosion, tiny nicks, scratches, and the like. Large cents in this condition are very valuable and should be carefully handled to maintain their status.

The description of wear for large cents covers that of the half-cent series.

The Eagle cents of 1856 through 1858 first show signs of wear upon the eagle's breast directly below the wing. The wing tip and eyebrow should also be examined. Some Eagle cents exist with very smooth tail feathers. This does not indicate wear, however, for many were lightly struck there.

Two-cent pieces are easy to detect for the "we" of the motto is the first item to go. Blurred horizontal lines in the shield are frequent, but these are not necessarily signs of wear, for many were coined in this manner.

The lock of hair above the ear first shows signs of wear on the three-cent nickel piece. These should also be closely examined for color, for soiled or discolored pieces are not desirable. Mint bloom should be evident upon these.

The Jefferson nickel wears first on Jefferson's cheekbone. On the reverse, just below the dome of Monticello, first signs of wear can be detected by a slight dulling or discoloration from the original glossy uncirculated look of the rest of the coin. These may be cleaned, but it is very difficult to erase this dulling effect.

Buffalo nickels are about the most difficult to identify in uncirculated condition. First, examine them for their original glossy mint bloom or color. If this is satisfactory, then examine the sharp edges of the coins for slight telltale hairlike scratches that will indicate circulation.

After this, closely examine the shoulder of the buffalo which will appear worn, for Buffalo nickels were coined in this manner, but examine the smooth shoulder for more telltale hairlike scratches. His hip, tail tip, and horn should be sharp. Next examine the cheek and just above the braid on the Indian's head for the same hairlike scratches. If the coin has no wear, no hairlike scratches on the above spots, and has its original mint bloom, you can assume it is a truly uncirculated coin.

The Liberty nickel first shows wear on the lock of hair over the temple and on the reverse highlights of the leaves in the wreath. The majority of Liberty nickels were struck very sharp, but blurred coinage is known in the years of 1911 and 1912.

Slight dulling of the original mint bloom on the highlights is the first sign of wear, as was the case with the Jefferson nickel.

The tiny crosslike emblem atop the shield of the Shield nickel shows evidence of wear first. On the reverse, examine the "5" for minute, hairlike scratches and signs of wear.

A great many of the three-cent silver pieces were not struck very sharply. Of the first design, these should have mint bloom and lack light hairlike scratches. The type II three-cent piece, from 1854 on, has sharply defined lines around the star. These are the first spots to wear although these tiny coins usually wear fairly evenly all over.

The first signs of wear on Liberty-Seated coins, whether they are half dimes, dimes, quarters, halves, or silver dollars, appear on the ear of the head (some are known to have been struck blurred, however), then on the thigh of Liberty Seated. The ribbon below the wreath, on the reverse of the dime and half dime, wears first. Quarters and halves first show wear on the eyebrow and upper beak of the eagle, then on the upper wing tips.

Bust-type quarters and halves wear first on the lock of hair near the ear, next on the clasp on the ribbon at the lower part of the bust. On the reverse, the eagle's upper bill and the top edges of the wings wear first. Some of these coins are known to have been lightly struck so the general appearance of the rest of the coin must be taken into consideration.

Telltale signs of wear first show up on the eagle's wing, right in the center of the coin, on a Peace dollar. On a Morgan dollar wear appears first on the eagle's breast and head. With both of these coins, the reverse seems to show wear a good deal faster than the obverse.

Barber quarters, halves, and dimes wear first on the obverse on the lock of hair over the forehead and temple directly below the word "Liberty." The cheek next shows discoloration and dulling. The reverse of the quarters and halves wears first directly above the eye of the eagle and the claws in his left talon.

The Liberty-Walking half-dollar coins first show wear on the breast of the eagle on the reverse. The head, breasts, and left leg of Miss Liberty are the next telltale signs. Franklin half dollars show their first sign of wear right in the center of the bell and on the cheek of Franklin. A slight dullness is the very first sign of wear.

Liberty-Standing quarters first show signs of wear on the knee of Miss Liberty. A slight flattening appears as the first telltale sign of wear. A number of these quarters were coined with flat heads, which appear worn, but this does not necessarily mean the coin is not uncirculated. Watch that knee for the first real signs of wear. On the reverse, the eagle's breast wears first, but not nearly as soon as the knee on the obverse. I have seen many beautiful (cleaned) Liberty-Standing quarters with full head, but with that telltale sign of wear on the knee. Don't be fooled by this one! Washington quarters first wear on the eagle's breast.

Now consider our early types of silver dollars. The type with flowing hair wears first on the eagle's breast and on the lock of hair directly behind the ear. The bust type, small eagle, on the reverse shows wear on the eagle's breast, on the obverse on the draped bust, directly above the first two digits of the date and to the extreme right bottom. The cheek wears next.

On Liberty Seated silver dollars, the first wear shows on the right thigh, closely followed by the forehead and the word "Liberty" on the shield; on the reverse, the eagle's beak and upper tips of wings wear first. On trade dollars, the knee, left breast, and head on the obverse show the first signs of wear; on the reverse the eagle's left leg, then upper tips of wings.

Commemorative coins should be examined carefully as many show wear, particularly in the early series. The first spots to wear are listed below:

Columbian Half Dollars
   Obverse: cheek and center lock of hair
   Reverse: center sail of ship; next, center of globes

New Rochelle, New York, 300th Anniversary
   Obverse: the calf's hip
   Reverse: highlights of the fleur-de-lis

Iowa Centennial
   Obverse: the eagle's breast
   Reverse: center columns, building, and the tower

Booker T. Washington Memorial
   Obverse: cheek and nose
   Reverse: highlights of center letters

Washington-Carver
  Obverse: the prominent cheek
  Reverse: the whole map of the United States
Isabella Quarter
  Obverse: cheek
  Reverse: head and left forearm
Lafayette Dollar
  Obverse: cheek of Washington
  Reverse: leg of equestrian; next, head
Panama-Pacific Exposition (1915)
  Obverse: head and left arm
  Reverse: eagle's breast
Lincoln, Illinois, Centennial
  Obverse: cheekbone
  Reverse: eagle's breast directly below forward part of left
  wing
Maine Centennial
  Obverse: fingers of left figure on scythe
  Reverse: ribbon holding wreath at bottom
Pilgrim Tercentenary
  Obverse: cheek, hatbrim, and book tip
  Reverse: high side of ship
Missouri Centennial
  Obverse: cheek and side of hat
  Reverse: pioneer's arm, both heads
Alabama Centennial
  Obverse: Kilby's cheek and forehead
  Reverse: eagle's breast directly above left leg
Grant Memorial
  Obverse: hair at temple
  Reverse: leaves of trees
Monroe Centennial
  Obverse: cheek and hair over temple
  Reverse: the faint figures in the maps of North and South
  America; examine coin for light hairlike scratches (This is a
  lightly struck coin hard to tell when slightly used.)
Huguenot-Walloon Tercentenary
  Obverse: outstanding rim and top of hat, also cape
  Reverse: hull of ship and shrouds

Obverse: fingers holding the gun
Reverse: point of block house at center

15.

PROOF COINS
MUST BE PERFECT

Proof coins are described by most publications as "Coins specially struck with mirror-like surface, for collectors, at Philadelphia only. Also sandblast and mat proof." But there is a lot more to them than that.

Today, they are very carefully struck to insure perfect specimens. Proofs are currently struck at San Francisco, and bear the "S" mint mark on the obverse. Until recently, they were struck by hand to insure perfection. At all times, the dies used were polished, as were the planchets. This gave the coins their mirror-like finish.

A genuine proof must be perfect. Its field, including the tiny spaces between letters and designs, must have this mirror-like finish. The highlights of the coin are sharp and have a "frosted" or "uncirculated" look, causing the designs to "stand out" from their mirror-like background. The edges are usually sharp and the coin is perfectly centered.

Proof coins are truly beautiful coins, whether they are of gold, silver, or copper. Sandblast or mat proofs have all the above qualifications, with the exception of the mirror-like finish; they have a dull velvety-type surface instead.

While the first regularly recognized issue of proofs for collectors commenced in 1858, proofs were coined before that time. The first early proofs were trial or experimental pieces to test designs and dies. Very few were struck and consequently they are very rare. These were usually not offered for sale to collectors but were more "presentation" pieces, samples of coinage, and so forth.

In 1858, when proofs were first offered for sale to collectors, the number struck was very small. Records of how many proofs were coined prior to 1877 are spotty, but from what information we have we can tell that the quantities were very small. By examining the records one can see how the interest in proof coins steadily increased as the years went by, popularity centering on the lower denominations.

During the nineteenth century, proof sets were offered as minor sets, complete sets, and those with gold. The minor sets were by far the most popular, the complete sets following second in popularity. Gold coins were not very popular in proof even though their premium cost was very little over the face value. Probably, this was due to the initial face-value investment involved. The coinage of proof double eagles ranged from only 20 to 158 proofs per year from 1865 to 1907.

Proofs were discontinued in 1915 and were not resumed again until 1936. The maximum number of proofs struck in 1915 for any denomination was around 1,000. The number struck in 1936 that can make up proof sets was around 3,300. This was quite an increase, but nothing like what occurred from 1936 to 1957 when 1,000,000 or so proof sets were coined.

From 1936 through 1942, proofs were not sold as "sets" only, as they are today. One could purchase any quantity of any denomination; you had to make up your own sets. From 1950 on, proofs have been sold as sets only.

Many "early strikes" of regular issue coins appear to be proofs, for the new dies frequently give the coins a mirror-like surface. This is often true with branch mint coins, but it must be remembered that no proofs were ever struck at any of the branch mints. While it is very difficult to detect these, it will be found that they never have the sharp, well struck edges of a genuine proof. The highlights are usually not sharp and the coin is not perfectly centered.

One frequently comes across attempts to fake proofs. Buffing will give an uncirculated coin a mirror-like finish, but this usually can be detected because the mirror-like finish is on the designs as well as the field. Even coins done more carefully, so that the designs are not buffed, can be detected by examining the tiny surfaces between the letters and designs where a buffer cannot get to. Of course the sharp edges of a genuine proof on such coins are lacking also.

Uncirculated coins that most frequently look like proof coins when they are not are: silver dollars, 1878 up, from all mints; Liberty-Seated halves, prior to 1890; quarters, prior to 1890; a few dimes in the 1870s; the 1866 nickel; the 1865 three-cent piece; gold dollars, particularly in the 1880s; and some of the later three-dollar gold pieces. With regard to the gold two-and-one-half-, five-, ten-, and twenty-dollar pieces, these sometimes are found with proof-like luster but are usually somewhat scratched, indicating contact with other coins.

Several of the scarcer, shorter issues, such as the four-dollar Stellas; the three-dollar coins of 1873, 1875, and 1876; the twenty-cent pieces of 1877 and 1878; the nickel three-cent pieces of 1877 and 1878; and the two-cent pieces of 1873, were only struck in proof, even though used specimens or "debased" proofs are occasionally found of these coins.

The three-dollar series, the nickel three-cent pieces, and the two-cent pieces were coins purely for collectors, to maintain a consecutive run of dates. The 1873 two-cent pieces and the 1877 and 1878 twenty-cent pieces struck for this reason turned out to be the last of the series.

The four-dollar Stellas were really trial or experimental pieces and were never coined for actual use.

Some denominations during the 1880s became unpopular for regular use but were coined for a decade or so in small quantities, probably to satisfy the collectors' demand for a complete "run of dates."

16.

BEWARE
OF COUNTERFEITS

The rapid price rise of nearly all United States coins has created a flood of counterfeits, altered dates, and other kinds of forgeries, many of which are so clever that the best experts are sometimes fooled. Below are those to watch out for:

Twenty-dollar gold pieces. All twenties are being coined, of the proper amount of gold, in foreign countries, designed to be sold to American collectors. They can be detected by examining the feathers in the center of the eagle on the reverse. These feathers are too sharply tooled. They also have a very proof-like, mirror-type surface. Beware of Liberty-Head types of rare dates, Philadelphia Mint, for the common branch mint coins are having the mint marks cleverly removed. Foreign made counterfeit Liberty Heads have very sharp milling—appear too new.

Ten-dollar gold pieces. Watch the 1858P; these are known to exist with their mint marks removed (branch mint). All tens are being coined in Europe at present.

Five-dollar gold pieces. Watch the 1909O as the O mint mark is known to have been added. All fives are being counterfeited.

Three-dollar gold pieces. There is a possibility that the later dates are being struck in Europe. They have a mirror-like appearance.

Four-dollar Stellas. Beware of gold-plated patterns struck in inferior metals and being sold as gold Stellas. The 1880 series coins are being struck presently in Europe.

Quarter eagles ($2.50). Both types, Indian Head and Liberty Head, are being struck in large quantities in Europe. They have the correct weight in gold and are very nearly perfect.

On fake Liberty Heads the head is too sharp, the edge of the coin is a trifle flat, and the milling is too sharp. These have a granular surface and they come in many dates. As to the Indian Heads, it is difficult to tell, but there again the milling is too fine and sharp.

Gold dollars. Coins of pretty nearly every date and mint have been copied. These, for the most part, have a granular surface, the beading on the edge tends to be too flat, the milling much too sharp, the deep-cut word "Liberty" on the headdress is usually sharp in the center and weak toward the end of each word. These are the new counterfeits struck in Europe and are very dangerous, being of the correct weight and fineness of gold. Old counterfeits are very easy to detect, for the gold content is inferior. The very rare 1854C has been faked by adding a sweated letter C to it; I have seen two of these in the last six months. Mint marks also are known to have been sweated to nearly all of the rarer branch mint gold dollars. In all denominations, these new European gold counterfeits are made by the centrifugal molding process and are very cleverly done.

Silver dollars. Removing the mint mark from an 1895O or S is done to make it the rare 1895P dollar. This coin was only struck in proof and, to be genuine, should be a perfect proof.

Half dollars. There are no outstanding new forgeries of halves recently other than the well-known addition of a star to the Grant Memorial half dollar. This is easily detected because the Grant stars were coined first. When the star was removed from the dies, a few minor defects were also corrected, namely slight bulges at the neck and below the nose. These always appear on the genuine Grant stars and never on the Grant without star. Counterfeit Grant stars also, at times, have a flattened spot on the reverse.

Quarter dollars. The 1923S, being rare, is being made by changing the 8 on a 1928S to a 3. Also, the mint mark on a 1913D is being retooled to look like an S. 1932 with a "D" cleverly added.

Dimes. Beware of the 1916D! I have seen these altered in all conditions; recently I saw a "good" one altered from a 1919D. Many have been faked by sweating a D cleverly on to a 1916P. These can be detected under a 20-power glass; close examination of the D will show some slight discoloration around the initial. Very frequently, the initial is out of its correct position. If sweated on, close examination will show indications of the base of the D tending to "round in" where it is attached to the coin, rather than being part of the planchet. A dealer recently had a roll of 1916D Unc. dimes offered to him. He picked the false "Ds" off of the coins and sent all back to the seller!

Another clever fraud is to take two dimes, a 1916P and a 1917D and mount them, with the 1916P obverse showing and the 1917D reverse showing, in an expensive plastic holder. In still another dangerous fraud, they punch the metal on the obverse out a little and fill it in so it is hardly noticeable; then with the bulge on the reverse they create a D. Very cleverly done! The celebrated 1894S has had S sweated on to the Philadelphia coin. I have not seen one of these, however, in thirty years.

Nickels. Watch 1950D. They are now cutting the tail off of 1959D to make it look like 1950D. Watch your 1937D three-legged nickels; they are now grinding off the one leg. To detect a genuine three-legged nickel, the point under the belly of the buffalo is long and very sharp; this does not appear on any other Buffalo nickel.

Watch this new angle. Dates are being put on dateless nickels by applying acids. The 1913 Liberty Head has for years been altered, either from a 1903 or a 1910. The 1895 nickels are being altered to 1885.

From 1866 through 1873 we had both the silver five-cent pieces of half dimes and the nickel five-cent pieces, two different types of this denomination. To top that off, the first Liberty nickels of 1883 did not have the word *cents* on them. After being gold-plated, they were frequently passed as five-dollar gold pieces, being the same size.

The twenty-cent coins were so similar to quarters that these two were frequently mistaken for each other. Last, but not least, a two-and-one-half-dollar gold piece is the same size as a cent. Many have been passed as cents, in error, due to this similarity.

I guess the five definitely different denominations we have today are the best.

Cents. This is the most popular series. The D is cleverly being ground off of the 1960 cents to make them P, small date only. 1937S cents are being retooled to look like 1931S. The 1922D cents are being changed to 1922 plain cents.

The 1914*D* is being made from an altered 1944*D*, with the first 4 being changed to a 1. The *D* is being sweated on the 1914*P* and the field is being ground down so that only the metal for the *D* is left. These are the hardest to identify, because one must examine the field around the letter to detect the concave depression. On 1909*S-VDB*, the letter *S* is being sweated to a common 1909*VDB*. (Initials of Victor D. Brenner, the coin's designer.) Indian cents apparently have not been tampered with. But watch the 1856 Eagle cent. These are commonly altered from an 1858.

Watch your coins; any coins valued at from a few dollars up are liable to be forged.

Be very careful of early rarities, particularly in Colonials, large cents and half cents; some of the electrotypes are so realistic they fool many an expert. An electrotype is a copper-plated lead piece made as an exact copy of the original rare coin. Electrotypes are considered by the government to be counterfeits if they are made in imitation of regular United States coinages. I know of an antique dealer who payed $110 for an electrotype of the rare 1792 Washington Large-Eagle half dollar, not knowing that it was a fake. A customer of ours recently purchased a collection of half cents from another collector for a high price, only to find that the 1796, 1831, 1852 cents—all very rare dates— were electrotypes. Those three coins, if genuine, would have been worth the major cost of the collection.

How can you detect electrotypes? Sometimes it is easy, other times not. First, an electrotype never has any lettering or milling on the edges; at least, I have never seen one that did. Second, sometimes one can detect a fine crack in the middle of the edge running around the coin where the two copper coatings have been pressed together; sometimes this has been eliminated by careful smoothing off of the edges. In any event, one can usually see one or the other: a slight crack or evidence of light smoothing on the edges of the coin. Third, usually an electrotype does not ring true. Its ring is sometimes remarkably near that of an original coin, however, in that the old copper coins do not ring very much anyway. Fourth, unless an electrotype has been very heavily plated, it usually can be bent with the fingers because the lead inside is soft. The antiquated system of biting a coin to test its genuineness may work if the plating is not too thick. Fifth, scraping the edge with a sharp knife usually will expose the lead under the thin copper plating; however, some electrotypes are so heavily plated that to scrape through seriously damages the coin if it turns out to be genuine. This is all I can suggest concerning electrotype detection, and I repeat, electrotypes are found mostly of early American Colonials, large cents.

17.

MINT ERRORS
AND THE RATING SCALE

Coins that are off-center or that have something wrong with them, formerly known as freaks, have now been given the name of *mint errors*. In the manufacture of coins, the mint carefully checks the new coins as they are coined, but occasionally a misstamped coin, or bill for that matter, manages to escape the eyes of the checkers and get into circulation. A good many of these mint errors are unique; others are quite common due to the ease with which certain errors occur and are overlooked. There is an association for mint-error collectors.

The difficulty of describing mint errors prompted the rating scale, which makes it easier to understand what the error is. For instance, on off-center coins, the clock is used as a guide. If you place the coin in front of you, the top would be numeral 12, and the circle of the coin would be divided into twelve equal spaces like the face of a clock. Thus, if you have an off-center Lincoln cent and the design is off to the right at about the number 3 of the clock, it is known as a "3 o'clock" off-center coin. If the coin is off at the bottom of the planchet, it is "6 o'clock" and so on around the face of the clock.

Degrees of off-center are figured in fractions of an inch. If the design is halfway off, showing half the planchet blank, and to the right, as described above in the first example, it is "3, ½ off." If the degree off is one quarter, showing three quarters of the coin design and one-fourth blank, it is known as "3, ¼ off." Therefore, the professional description of the last coin is: Lincoln cent 1911P ¼ O.C. in 3 o'clock.

Coins slightly off-center, or eclipsed (a circular piece out of the edge of the planchet at some spot), are the most common mint errors. This does not mean that all are, however. I recently had a large cent with the rare date 1811 in almost uncirculated condition which was off-center about ⅛ at 2 on the obverse. The unusual thing about this cent was that, while it was the same amount off on the reverse, the design was *incused*, or cut in, rather than raised up and very sharp. This most likely was the result of two planchets being struck at once and the design of one cent being impressed in reverse on the other. The combination of errors, plus the rarity of the coin and its condition, make it very rare.

A popular type of mint error is the cent that is struck on a silver planchet. This can happen when a dime planchet gets mixed up with the cent ones; consequently the cent design is struck on the silver dime planchet. Many persons think these are very rare, but there are more of them than one realizes. A count made recently indicated that there were approximately forty-five known silver cents. They are frequently quoted as being worth thousands of dollars, but auction records indicate a bonafide sale of one of these at $700. Most dealers shy from this coin.

One of the most sought after and popular mint errors is the copper cent of 1943, the year they made steel cents only. Many people claim to have these copper cents, but close inspection shows that nearly all are fakes. It is very easy to copper-plate a steel cent, but this can be detected by giving it a magnet test. If the cent adheres to the magnet, you may be certain there is a steel cent under the plating.

Errors in paper money are also ardently sought. The commonest errors are bills that are slightly off-center. Also common are bills that had the paper folded slightly so that there is a "white spot" across some part of the note. Probably the most desirable are notes that have one denomination on one side, and another on the other. I recently saw one of these on exhibition, a one dollar reverse and a five dollar obverse.

Other very unusual mint errors are bills with composite folds that give a white, unprinted, accordion effect; notes printed heavily on one side of the reverse or obverse with ink fading to nothing on the other side; and notes with signatures and numbers upside down. All these are very rare. And one must remember that mint errors, as well as all coins, must be in perfect condition to demand the best prices. Even though the error is an unusual one, if the note has been used a lot, its value is one-tenth what it would have been had it been crisp-new.

18.
SHALL I CLEAN
MY COINS?

This age-old question has been bothering collectors and dealers for a long time. Originally, the cleaning of coins was taboo and those that first attempted cleaning did their best to have the coins they cleaned look as much as possible as if they had not been cleaned. Today, well-cleaned coins are accepted as readily as (and sometimes more readily than) those that have been kept in their original state, with exceptions. The coins cleaned and the cleaner used determine the desirability of the coin in question.

Never clean a badly worn coin of any kind. In the first place, it is a waste of time and, cleaning a coin that is in a condition inferior to very fine will never enhance it.

PROOFS

Proofs in gold seldom if ever will need cleaning. In silver they frequently become tarnished and are preferred so by collectors. If the tarnish is not too dark, Silver Dip purchased in your local supermarket will brighten them without scratching. Don't leave the coin in the dip more than five seconds or so, and rinse immediately with water. Dry with a soft cleansing tissue. Proof nickels will react favorably to the foregoing treatment.

For bronze and copper coins, leave proofs alone. A nicely toned proof cent is more desirable than one that is brilliantly cleaned. If there are specks or corrosion spots on the coin, it will then have to be cleaned, but it is questionable whether the spots will come off and, if they do, whether the cleaning will not harm the proof surface. Silver proofs that have been cleaned seem to be more desirable to the collector than uncleaned ones because detection is difficult and they like their proofs bright in silver. In copper, however, toned ones are more desirable, for the brightness of a cleaned copper coin is easily detected.

UNCIRCULATED COINS

Gold uncirculated coins rarely need cleaning. At times it might be advisable to wash them gently with Ivory soap and warm water. Silver coins, if lightly tarnished, can be brightened nicely by using Silver Dip as suggested for the proofs (a five-second dip and then a quick rinse). If heavily tarnished, silver coins should be cleaned as follows: make a paste of bicarbonate of soda and water. Do not use the ordinary inexpensive brand of soda available in grocery stores, but use the better grade found in drugstores; the texture of the cheaper brand is coarse and may scratch, whereas the better brand is smoother and does not tend to scratch as much. Be certain your fingers are soft and smooth with no nicks or scratches on the skin. It is a good idea to soak them a minute or so in warm water to soften. Then rub the coin gently with the paste until all tarnish is gone. Don't forget the edges.

COPPER COINS

Large cents or half cents in copper should never be cleaned. Indian Heads and Lincolns should not be cleaned if they are naturally brilliant or red. If they are toned down so that only a slight amount of red or no red shows, it probably is better to clean them today than leave them as they are, for a dark uncirculated cent of the small size does not seem to be as desirable as a cleaned brilliant one. A product called Care can be used on copper and bronze coins. This does not change their color but removes grease and dirt and gives them a glossy protective coating. Brilliantize does a good job even removing spots, provided one follows instructions. The cent will be very bright when finished and really nice looking, far superior to what it formerly looked like. Specks and spots can also be removed if they are on the coin. There is a tendency for copper coins to tone down more rapidly after cleaning than they would naturally, and this should be kept in mind.

VERY FINE AND EXTREMELY FINE COINS

Gold rarely needs cleaning. Ivory soap and warm water should do, if it is absolutely necessary. Silver pieces can be cleaned with bicarbonate of soda following the instructions given for uncirculated silver pieces. This usually improves the looks of the coin. Copper or bronze coins in this condition should never be cleaned. They look better in their natural state.

Silver will tarnish very quickly, particularly if exposed to air and other chemicals that affect it. It is difficult to believe that brilliant uncirculated or proof coins as old as a hundred or more years could possibly have lasted all that while without ever having been tarnished. It is my opinion that nearly all choice silver coins have been cleaned at some time or other and perhaps many times. It hasn't hurt them; in fact, had tarnish been allowed to increase, the coin would finally have become black and the tarnish would have had a permanently bad effect on the condition of the coin. The surface of very badly tarnished silver coins begins to be eaten away and can never be brought back, the corrosive quality of the tarnish having deteriorated the value of the coin.

Many collectors of large cents prefer their uncirculated specimens in a rich brown or steel color that is acquired naturally through the years. The film that gives these cents this fine glossy surface is a protection preventing the annoying corrosion spots that so frequently appear on cents that are red or brilliant. This is not the case with collectors of small cents; with this series they want them brilliant or red even though these, too, are subject to the same annoying spots: I wonder when small-cent collectors will follow the large-cent collectors and will appreciate the value of rich, colored small cents, rather than the brilliant ones that are subject to deterioration.

19.
HOW TO SELL
A COIN COLLECTION

For some time I have wanted to write about the sale of coins, how to go about it and how to get what they are worth. A reader of mine wanted to know what a widow should do to sell a coin collection. This is a very difficult problem for an inexperienced person.

How to go about selling a collection depends upon the value of the collection. If it is a matter of a few hundred dollars, an outright sale is the best. If it is a collection running in excess of several thousand dollars, the story is entirely different.

In the first place, every collector should make arrangements for the sale of his collection while he is still collecting. Since he has dealt (and is dealing) with many large dealers he is in a good position to form an opinion as to whom he would trust his collection with and whom he would not. This information should be passed on to his heirs. The sale of a collection of size has to depend upon the absolute trust in the dealer purchasing it or handling its sale. There are many honest dealers in this country, but there are a few others who will use all kinds of slick tricks to get the most for the least amount of money.

When death occurs, the first step is that the collection will have to be appraised for both state and federal inheritance taxes. Appraisals can be done on both a low wholesale or a high retail valuation. Expert appraisers should give both the wholesale and retail valuation. For inheritance tax purposes, a figure between the two should be used.

It is advisable not to keep the appraisal valuations too low for this purpose, because when the collection is sold there would then be a much higher capital gains tax which would cost more than paying a higher inheritance tax.

The choice of an appraiser is very important. Get the best and to your knowledge the most honest. Pay his fee rather than accept a free appraisal. This keeps you from being obligated to any one person in the event of sale and should get you a better appraisal. There is a great temptation for appraisers to keep values down low on a free appraisal with an eye to purchasing the collection. An appraiser should be a disinterested party, not the prospective purchaser of the collection or his agent.

Next we come to the manner of selling, whether it is outright for cash or at auction. If sold outright, one should expect to receive between 50 and 70 percent of the retail sales value. This does not mean the guide book or catalog value, but the amount the coins would actually sell for. This will vary considerably from guide book prices depending upon what the collection contains.

Proofs and key rarities usually retail for as much as full guide book prices, and in many instances for considerably above these valuations. Extreme rarities in great demand can go at two, three, and even ten times catalog value. Circulated coins of the more common variety, even ordinary uncirculated coins, rarely sell up to guide book valuations; usually they sell at from 20 to 40 percent under them.

The discount paid from retail values of 50 to 70 percent depends upon the type of material the collection contains and the amount of work involved in selling the material. One must always remember that a dealer is in business to earn his living and is entitled to his profits for his efforts.

Now we come to selling at auction. This is the manner in which all of the leading collections are sold. It has advantages and disadvantages. While cash advances on a consignment can usually be gotten, the final settlement is usually slower than a cash sale because of the length of time it takes to handle the sale. The advantages are first that the auctioneer is very anxious to realize as much as possible for the collection. The more he can realize, the more his commission will be. He will catalog the coins to their best advantage, and hidden or unknown rarities that otherwise might not be mentioned in an outright sale will be featured in order to get the most for the collection.

Surprises also occur which even conscientious dealers might not expect when purchasing outright. A coin which a dealer would normally purchase for full guide book price, suspecting it would sell for considerably more, sold recently at auction for three times guide book price!

Other advantages of the auction method include a complete published and printed record in the catalog of the collection. Also a complete printed and priced list is made of what the collection brought for every lot. And lastly, when desired, the name of the collector is published in conjunction with the sale of the collection, crediting him for his efforts in compiling it.

The auction method does take time. It will take the cataloger about a month to prepare the catalog. A month should be allowed to let the printer print it and get it into the mail. Then four to six weeks should be allowed for the collectors and dealers to send in their bids. At the termination of the sale, another month should be allowed for payments to come on the lots sold. So one can expect to have settlement in full thirty days after the termination of the auction sale. Insofar as one must wait six months for appraisal for inheritance tax purposes in order to have the profit from the sale come under capital gains rather than income tax, the length of time the auction method takes is no disadvantage.

The fee an auctioneer gets for his service ranges between 10 and 25 percent of the prices realized and should include all costs, insurance, advertising, printing, etc.

Inexperienced people sometimes fear the auction method, being afraid the coins will go for a price way below value. This is not the case. Auctioneers who run large, nationwide sales cover the market so completely, both as to dealers and collectors, there is little opportunity for any lot to go for a ridiculous price. Sometimes an unpopular item sells at a price that appears to be quite cheap, but that is really what it is worth.

The best auctions are those run by dealers who have specialized in this selling method for many years, for in so doing they have built up a clientele and a reputation that encourages good bidding. The best sales are a combination of mail bids and then a public sale commenced with the high mail bid. This system brings the best prices, encourages competition, and the prices realized are publicly announced.

WATCH OUT FOR THE FOLLOWING
WHEN SELLING FOR CASH:

Downgrading. Downgrading is listing or grading a coin as inferior to what it actually is. I know of a collection of beautiful proofs that was purchased several years ago as "uncirculated" by an unscrupulous dealer.

Disinterest. A common practice among "slickys" is to push the choice pieces aside, concentrate on a few common ones, pay a good price for these, and get the real rare coins for a song.

Use of fear. Many a gold coin has been purchased, under threat of penalty to own (a law which is nonexistent), at as low as half face value.

Omission. Lots of rare coins have been sold for a song simply by the purchaser forgetting to mention that they are rare and buying a group as a "lot."

WATCH OUT FOR THE FOLLOWING
WHEN SELLING AT AUCTION:

High cash advances, too-low commission charges. High cash advances and too-low commission charges are inducements that are likely to work to your disadvantage. They are come-ons to get your coins.

Local club auctions. These are honest sales but they do not have the number of bidders necessary to bring good prices. They are usually started with a minimum bid which causes a good percentage of the items to be returned unsold, as no one will take up the bidding. On the other hand, a majority of those that are sold go for the minimum, which may be very low.

Part-time auctioneers. They do not have the clientele or experience to do a good job on your collection. It takes many years of experience to catalog correctly, build a reputation, and get lots of active bidding from both dealers and collectors.

Choice of a dealer to buy outright or sell at auction. Every dealer will tell you how great and honest he is. Some will knock their competitors (beware of these!). The best test if you don't know any is to check his references, his bank, and his Dun & Bradstreet ratings. Also, get the names of half a dozen other collectors who have actually done business with him and find out whether they were satisfied.

It's not very nice to consign a collection to a dealer for outright sale or auction and have to wait and wait to get paid. If it's a cash sale, don't take it in installments; that can go on for years, the cream may then be gone, and you may have to take back what's left that the dealer couldn't sell.

Check the promptness with which your auctioneer will pay. We know a collector who sold an $80,000 collection at auction and had to travel 700 miles each month to get $10,000 each trip, when he should have been paid outright in thirty days.

20.

COIN VALUES ARE DETERMINED
BY DEMAND AND CONDITION

New collectors take up the hobby of coin collecting every day. Older coins disappear from circulation very quickly and the supply coming into the market from the break-up of collections cannot keep pace with the demand that comes from ever greater numbers of collectors of American coins. Thus, the demand for these coins grows while the supply diminishes. The result has been a steadily rising level in the value of American coins.

Besides rarity, however, there is another factor that affects a coin's value, namely, its state of preservation or condition. Collectors will often pay many times as much for a coin in superior condition than for a specimen that is just average.

The prices listed in this book are, for the most part, for "fine" coins. A "fine" coin is one that shows a reasonable amount of wear but is still a desirable coin. The basic outline is still clear but much of the fine detail is worn away. All lettering should be legible. The next grade below this is "very good," a much worn but not altogether unattractive coin. A coin in this condition should be free of serious gouges or other mutilations but it may be somewhat scratched from use. A coin that is rated only "good" is really a minimum condition coin. The date and mint mark would be legible and the major portions of the design distinguishable. "Fair" indicates a badly worn coin that is usually not acceptable to a collector. "Fair" coins are generally used as "space fillers," only until such time as a better coin can be acquired.

The grade above "fine" is "very fine," a coin on which the design is still quite clear, and which over all shows the very slightest amount of wear. An "extremely fine" coin shows the slightest signs of wear or rubbing only on the very highest points of the design. "Uncirculated" indicates a coin absolutely without wear. Above "uncirculated" is "proof," a coin which is a special coin with a mirror-like surface especially minted for collectors. The "proof" coin must be absolutely perfect.

There is no iron-bound rule as to values but the following pages should give you an *approximate* idea of what your coins are worth. The values shown are the prices the dealers charge when they sell coins. If a "fine" coin as listed in this book is listed at $10, you can expect dealers to pay you between 50 and 70 percent of the price shown. This will, of course, depend upon how badly the dealer needs the coin or coins. Dealers usually carry a large stock of coins and cannot be expected to pay high prices for those items that they have a lot of. On the other hand, if he needs your coin badly, he often will pay record prices.

Part Two:

THE COINS LISTED

ABBREVIATIONS USED
IN THE COIN VALUE LISTS

Unc.—Uncirculated
Ex. Fine—Extremely Fine
V. Fine—Very Fine
V. Good—Very Good

More detailed information about minor varieties can be found in the following books:

A Guide Book of U.S. Coins, Whitman Publishing Co. General information.
Miller-Ryder, *The State Coinages of New England.* Colonial Coins.
Dr. Edward Maris, *New Jersey Cents.* Colonial Coins.
Sydney P. Noe, *The New England and Willow Tree Coinages of Massachusetts.* Colonial Coins.
S. S. Crosby, *Cents and Half Cents of 1793.*
Gilbert Elder, *U.S. Half Cents.*
Wm. H. Sheldon, *Penny Whimsey.* Large cents.
D. W. Valentine, *U.S. Half Dimes.*
J. W. Haseltine, *Type table of U.S. Dollars, Halves and Quarters.*
M. H. Bolender, *Silver Dollars 1794–1804.*

21.

COLONIAL COINS BEFORE THE
DECLARATION OF INDEPENDENCE: 1652–1776

MASSACHUSETTS

NEW ENGLAND PIECES
Shilling

	Good	Fine	
NE Shilling	4,000.00	8,000.00	—
NE Sixpence (Very rare) 6 known	—	—	—
NE Threepence (2 known, very rare)	—	—	—

WILLOW TREE PIECES (1652)

Willow Tree Shilling	5,000.00	10,000.00	—
Willow Tree Sixpence	5,000.00	11,500.00	—
Willow Tree Threepence (3 known, very rare)	—	—	—

OAK TREE PIECES (1652)

Oak Tree Shilling	500.00	1,100.00	—
Oak Tree Sixpence	700.00	1,300.00	—
Oak Tree Threepence	550.00	1,300.00	—
Oak Tree Twopence (1662)	450.00	1,100.00	—

PINE TREE PIECES (1652)

Pine Tree Shilling, Large Planchet	350.00	900.00	—
Pine Tree Shilling, Small Planchet	325.00	750.00	—
Pine Tree Sixpence	375.00	800.00	—
Pine Tree Threepence	325.00	700.00	—

MARYLAND (1658)

LORD BALTIMORE COINAGE

Shilling	1,250.00	3,500.00	—
Sixpence	875.00	2,200.00	—
Fourpence	1,250.00	3,250.00	—

NEW JERSEY

MARK NEWBY COINAGE

St. Patrick Halfpence	125.00	300.00	—
St. Patrick Farthing with Brass Plug on Obverse	75.00	150.00	—
St. Patrick Farthing without Brass Plug	75.00	150.00	—
St. Patrick Farthing, Silver	1,000.00	2,250.00	—

FLORIDA TOKEN

	Good	Fine	Unc.
(1688) Florida, James II Plantation Token, 1/24 part real—Pewter	90.00	225.00	900.00

CAROLINA ELEPHANT TOKENS

	Good	Fine	Ex. Fine
1694 PROPRIETERS (3 known)	—	—	—
1694 PROPRIETERS	900.00	3,000.00	—
(1694) Halfpenny GOD PRESERVE LONDON (Thick Planchet)	60.00	125.00	325.00
(1694) Halfpenny GOD PRESERVE LONDON (Thin Planchet)	75.00	150.00	375.00
(1694) Halfpenny GOD PRESERVE LONDON (Diagonals in center of shield)	100.00	200.00	700.00
(1694) Halfpenny, similar. Variety with sword in second quarter of shield instead of first (rare)	—	—	—
(1694) Halfpenny LON DON	500.00	1,000.00	—

NEW ENGLAND

1694 NEW ENGLAND (Very rare)	—	—	—

FRENCH COLONIES

1721 Mint Mark B, Sou	50.00	110.00	—
1721 Mint Mark H, Sou	25.00	60.00	—
1722 Sou	25.00	60.00	—
1722 Sou, 2 over 1	50.00	110.00	—
1767 Sou	35.00	90.00	—
1767 Sou Counterstamp "R.F."	15.00	40.00	—

WILLIAM WOOD'S COINAGE

ROSA AMERICANA

	Good	Fine	Ex Fine
Twopence (no date)	60.00	250.00	600.00
1722 Twopence, Period after REX	50.00	100.00	300.00
1722 Twopence, No Period after REX	50.00	100.00	300.00
1722 Penny UTILE DULCI	50.00	100.00	250.00
1722 Penny VTILE DVLCI	40.00	95.00	200.00
1722 Halfpenny D.G. REX ROSA AMERI. UTILE DULCI	40.00	125.00	225.00
1722 Halfpenny DEI GRATIA REX UTILE DULCI	30.00	75.00	200.00
1722 Halfpenny VTILE DVLCI	—	—	—
1723 Twopence	75.00	150.00	350.00
1723 Penny	50.00	90.00	200.00
1723 Halfpenny	45.00	85.00	200.00
1723 Halfpenny Uncrowned Rose (rare)	—	—	—
1724 Penny (rare)	—	—	—
1724 Penny (Undated) ROSA:SINE: SPINA. (3 known)	—	—	—

HIBERNIA

1722 Halfpenny, First Type, Harp at Left	12.00	40.00	150.00
1722 Halfpenny, Second Type, Harp at Right	12.00	55.00	175.00
1722 Farthing (rare)	—	—	—

	Good	Fine	Ex. Fine
1723 Halfpenny	10.00	25.00	80.00
1723 over 22 Halfpenny	17.50	65.00	175.00
1723 Farthing	12.50	30.00	125.00
1724 Halfpenny	12.50	35.00	170.00
1724 Farthing	20.00	70.00	185.00

HIGLEY COPPERS

	Fair	Good	—
1737 THE•VALVE•OF•THREE•PENCE.—3 Hammers CONNECTICVT	4,000.00	8,500.00	—
1737 THE•VALVE•OF•THREE•PENCE.—3 Hammers—I•AM•GOOD•COPPER	5,000.00	10,000.00	—
1737 VALUE•ME•AS•YOU•PLEASE—3 Hammers—I•AM•GOOD•COPPER	4,000.00	7,000.00	—
1737 VALVE•ME•AS•YOU•PLEASE—3 Hammers—I•AM•GOOD•COPPER (rare)	—	—	—
(1737) VALUE•ME•AS•YOU•PLEASE—Broad Axe—J•CUT•MY•WAY•THROUGH	5,000.00	10,000.00	—
(1737) Similar, Wheel Design (Unique)	—	—	—
1739 VALUE•ME•AS•YOU•PLEASE—Broad Axe— J•CUT•MY•WAY•THROUGH	6,000.00	16,000.00	—

VOCE POPULI

	Good	Fine	—
1700 Halfpenny	—	—	—
1760 Halfpenny	20.00	50.00	100.00
1760 Halfpenny VOOE POPULI	35.00	90.00	150.00
1760 Farthing Large Letters	100.00	350.00	1,000.00
1760 Farthing Small Letters (rare)	—	—	—

PITT TOKEN

	Good	Fine	Ex. Fine
1766 Halfpenny	100.00	200.00	475.00
1766 Farthing (rare)	—	—	—

VIRGINIA

	Good	Fine	Unc.
1773 Halfpenny, Period after GEORGIUS	22.50	45.00	250.00
1773 Halfpenny, No period after GEORGIUS	30.00	75.00	350.00

22

STATE COINAGE

CONNECTICUT CENTS

	Good	Fine	V. Fine
1785 Bust Right	20.00	75.00	150.00
1785 Bust Left	125.00	250.00	500.00
1786 Bust Right	40.00	85.00	150.00
1786 Bust Left	20.00	60.00	125.00
1786 Draped Bust	50.00	125.00	250.00
1787 Mailed Bust Right	50.00	150.00	300.00
1787 Mailed Bust Left	20.00	60.00	125.00
1787 Draped Bust Left	15.00	30.00	65.00
1788 Mailed Bust Right	20.00	60.00	135.00
1788 Mailed Bust Left	15.00	50.00	115.00
1788 Draped Bust Left	15.00	50.00	85.00

(Note: There are many minor varieties of Connecticut Cents.)

MASSACHUSETTS

	Good	Fine	Ex. Fine
1787 Cent, Arrows in Right Talon (Ex. rare)	—	—	—
1787 Cent, Arrows in Left Talon	20.00	40.00	175.00
1787 Cent, Horn (Die Break) from Eagle's Head	20.00	45.00	225.00
1787 Half Cent	25.00	60.00	190.00
1788 Cent	25.00	50.00	190.00
1788 Half Cent	30.00	60.00	250.00

NEW HAMPSHIRE

1776 New Hampshire Penny (Very rare)	—	—	—

NEW JERSEY CENTS

	Good	Fine	V. Fine
1786 IMMUNIS COLUMBIA (Very rare)	—	—	—
1786 Date under Plow Handle (Very rare)	—	—	—
1786 No Coulter	100.00	300.00	700.00
1786 Narrow or Wide Shield	22.50	55.00	125.00
1787 Small or Large Planchet	20.00	45.00	90.00
1787 Outlined Shield	15.00	40.00	90.00
1787 Pluribs instead of Pluribus	30.00	90.00	200.00
1788 Horse head Right	20.00	40.00	90.00
1788 Horse head Left	65.00	175.00	300.00

(Note: There are many minor varieties of New Jersey Cents.)

NEW YORK CENTS

	Good	Fine	V. Fine
1786 NON VI VIRTUTE VICI	2,500.00	5,000.00	9,500.00
1787 Excelsior Cent, Eagle Right	450.00	1,100.00	3,250.00
1787 Excelsior Cent, Eagle Left	425.00	1,000.00	3,000.00
1787 Excelsior Cent, Large Eagle (Very rare)	—	—	—
1787 Excelsior, Indian	1,500.00	3,000.00	5,500.00
1787 Excelsior George Clinton	3,000.00	6,000.00	12,000.00
1787 Indian, Eagle on Globe	2,500.00	3,500.00	6,000.00
1787 IMMUNIS COLUMBIA	150.00	300.00	700.00
1787 NOVA-EBORAC, Figure Left	50.00	150.00	325.00
1787 NOVA-EBORAC, Figure Right	55.00	165.00	350.00
1787 NOVA-EBORAC, Small Head	300.00	650.00	1,500.00
1787 NOVA-EBORAC, Large Head	225.00	400.00	800.00

VERMONT CENTS

	Good	Fine	
1785 IMMUNE COLUMBIA	1,500.00	4,200.00	—
1785 Mountain Scene, VERMONTS	100.00	375.00	—
1785 Mountain Scene, VERMONTIS	115.00	425.00	—
1786 Mountain Scene, VERMONTENSIUM	100.00	275.00	—
1786 Baby Head, Bust Right	150.00	600.00	—
1786 Bust Left	60.00	250.00	—
1787 Bust Left (Rare)	—	—	—
1787 Bust Right	45.00	150.00	—
1787 BRITANNIA on Reverse	40.00	135.00	—
1788	40.00	150.00	—
1788 GEORGIUS III REX	125.00	400.00	—

EXPERIMENTAL COINS

CONTINENTAL DOLLAR

	Good	Fine	Ex. Fine
1776 CURENCY, Pewter	1,250.00	3,500.00	7,500.00
1776 CURENCY, Brass (Very rare)	—	—	—
1776 CURENCY, Silver (Very rare)	—	15,000.00	—
1776 CURENCY, Pewter	1,350.00	4,500.00	9,000.00
1776 CURENCY, Pewter, E.G. Fecit	1,300.00	4,000.00	8,500.00

	Good	Fine	Ex. Fine
1776 CURRENCY, Silver, E.G. Fecit (Very rare)	—	—	—
1776 CURRENCEY, Pewter (Very rare)	—	—	—

NOVA CONSTELLATIO (SILVER)

	Good	Fine	Ex. Fine
1783 MARK (1000), Silver (Unique)	—	—	—
1783 QUINT (500), Silver—Type 1 (Unique)	—	—	—
1783 QUINT (500), Silver—Type 2 (Unique)	—	—	—
1783 Bit (100), Silver (2 known)	—	—	—

NOVA CONSTELLATIO CENTS

	Good	Fine	Ex. Fine
1783 CONSTELLATIO, Small U.S.	20.00	50.00	150.00
1783 CONSTELLATIO, Large U.S.	25.00	75.00	175.00
1783 CONSTELATIO, Blunt Rays	20.00	60.00	150.00
1785 CONSTELATIO, Blunt Rays	22.50	65.00	190.00
1785 CONSTELLATIO, Pointed Rays	20.00	50.00	125.00
1786 CONSTELLATIO (Very rare)	—	—	—

IMMUNE COLUMBIA CENTS

	Good	Fine	V. Fine
1785 CONSTELLATIO (Very rare)	—	—	—
1785 CONSTELATIO (Very rare) Known in Copper and Gold	—	—	—
1785 George III Obverse	1,500.00	4,000.00	—
1785 VERMON AUCTORI Obverse	1,250.00	3,500.00	—

CONFEDERATIO CENTS

	Good	Fine	Ex. Fine
1785 Stars in Large or Small Circle (All very rare)	—	—	—

THE FUGIO CENTS

	Good	Fine	Ex. Fine
1787 Club Rays	50.00	180.00	450.00

Pointed Rays

1787 UNITED above STATES below (rare)	—	—	—
1787 UNITED STATES at sides of circle	40.00	80.00	200.00

1787 STATES UNITED at sides of circle	35.00	90.00	200.00

(Note: There are several minor varieties of the Fugio Cents.)

MISCELLANEOUS TOKENS

RHODE ISLAND SHIP TOKEN

1778 Wreath below Ship	110.00	250.00	950.00
1778 No wreath	110.00	250.00	800.00

NORTH AMERICAN TOKEN

	Good	Fine	V. Fine
1781	10.00	30.00	90.00

GEORGIUS TRIUMPHO TOKEN

1783 GEORGIUS TRIUMPHO	50.00	125.00	350.00

J. CHALMERS

ANNAPOLIS, MARYLAND

1783 Shilling—Birds, Long or Short Worm	400.00	1,100.00	—
1783 Shilling—Rings (Ex. rare)	—	—	—
1783 Sixpence, Small Date	800.00	1,800.00	—
1783 Sixpence, Large Date	550.00	1,400.00	—
1783 Threepence	425.00	950.00	—

THE BAR CENT

	Good	Fine	Ex. Fine
Undated (1785) Bar Cent	250.00	650.00	—

AUCTORI PLEBIS TOKEN

	Good	Fine	V. Fine
1787	50.00	100.00	225.00

BRASHER'S DOUBLOONS

1787 "E.B." on Breast or Wing (All very rare)	—	—	—

THE MOTT TOKEN

	Good	Fine	Ex. Fine
1789 Mott Token, Thick Planchet	45.00	110.00	225.00
1789 Mott Token, Thin Planchet	60.00	160.00	475.00

STANDISH BARRY BALTIMORE, MARYLAND

1790 Threepence (Very rare)	—	—	—

ALBANY CHURCH PENNY

(1790)	1,500.00	2,500.00	—

KENTUCKY TOKEN

	V. Good	V. Fine	Unc.
Cent (1792-94) Plain Edge	30.00	70.00	225.00
Cent, Engrailed Edge	110.00	240.00	650.00
Cent, Lettered Edge	50.00	125.00	300.00

FRANKLIN PRESS CENT

	Good	Fine	Unc.
1794	30.00	65.00	165.00

TALBOT ALLUM & LEE CENTS

1794 With NEW YORK	20.00	50.00	400.00
1794 Without NEW YORK	125.00	400.00	—
1795	10.00	30.00	275.00

MYDDLETON TOKENS

	Good	Fine	Unc.
1796 Copper. Proof only	—	—	5,500.00
1796 Silver. Proof only	—	—	4,500.00

WASHINGTON PIECES

	Good	Fine	Ex. Fine
1783 WASHINGTON & INDEPENDENCE Small Military bust	12.50	35.00	125.00
1783 Same, Engrailed Edge	20.00	50.00	180.00
1783 Large Military bust	10.00	25.00	110.00
1783 Draped bust	10.00	25.00	110.00
1783 Draped bust with button	25.00	75.00	225.00
1783 Restrike in Copper. Proof only. Plain Edge	—	Proof	225.00
1783 Restrike in Copper. Proof only. Engrailed Edge	—	Proof	125.00
1783 Restrike in Silver. Proof only. Engrailed Edge	—	Proof	350.00
1783 UNITY STATES	20.00	50.00	125.00
(1783) Double Head Cent	20.00	50.00	150.00
1784 Ugly Head (Very rare)	—	—	—
1791 Cent, Small Eagle	60.00	125.00	600.00
1791 Large Eagle	50.00	100.00	575.00
1792 WASHINGTON PRESIDENT	2,000.00	5,000.00	—
(1792) WASHINGTON BORN VIRGINIA	1,250.00	2,000.00	—

	Good	Fine	Unc.
1792 Roman Head (Rare)———			
1795 Grate Cent, Lettered edge	150.00	250.00	750.00
1795 Grate Cent, Reeded edge	20.00	40.00	250.00

WASHINGTON PENNIES AND HALFPENNIES

	Good	Fine	Unc.
(1795) Penny, Lettered edge "LIBERTY & SECURITY"	40.00	115.00	950.00
1791 LIVERPOOL HALF PENNY	200.00	600.00	2,000.00

	Good	Fine	Ex. Fine
1793 Ship Halfpenny	40.00	75.00	350.00
1795 Liberty & Security Halfpenny, Plain edge	50.00	150.00	325.00
1795 Halfpenny, Lettered edge	30.00	75.00	100.00
1795 Halfpenny, Edge "AN ASYLUM FOR THE OPPRESSED OF ALL NATIONS"	90.00	250.00	550.00
1795 NORTH WALES Halfpenny	60.00	200.00	—
SUCCESS Token Large, Plain & Reeded edge	50.00	125.00	500.00
SUCCESS Token Small, Plain & Reeded edge	50.00	125.00	700.00

WASHINGTON HALF DOLLARS

	Good	Fine	
1792 Silver Half Dollar (Very rare)	—	—	—
1792 Silver, Ornamental edge (Very rare)	—	—	—
1792 Copper	1,500.00	4,000.00	—
1792 Copper, Ornamental edge	—	—	—

23.

FIRST MINT ISSUES

	Good	Fine	Unc.
1792 DISME known in Silver and Copper (Very rare)	—	—	—

	Good	Fine	Ex. Fine
1792 HALF DISME, Silver	1,250.00	2,500.00	8,500.00
1792 HALF DISME, Copper (Very rare)	—	—	—
1792 Silver Center Cent (Very rare)	—	—	—
1792 BIRCH CENT (Very rare)	—	—	—

24.

HALF-CENT PIECES— 1793–1857

Note: All half cents in *fair* to *about good* condition (i.e. unmutilated but worn) are valued at about one-third of the good column.

LIBERTY CAP TYPE

1793   1794–1797

	Mintage in Thousands	Good	Fine	V.Fine
1793..	35	1,500.00	2,500.00	3,000.00
1794..	82	150.00	300.00	600.00
1795 Lettered Edge, Pole to Cap........	26	150.00	300.00	600.00
1795 Plain Edge, No Pole to Cap........	109	150.00	300.00	600.00
1796 Plain Edge, Pole.....................	5	1,250.00	2,500.00	6,000.00
1796 Plain Edge, No Pole.................	1	2,000.00	4,500.00	9,500.00
1797 Plain Edge, All Kinds..............	119	150.00	300.00	550.00
1797 Lettered Edge........................	—	250.00	750.00	1,500.00

DRAPED BUST TYPE

1800...	212	15.00	30.00	50.00
1802 2 over 0, Rev. of 1800, All Kinds................................	14	550.00	1,200.00	2,000.00
1802 2 over 0, New Rev....................	—	135.00	300.00	550.00

	Mintage in Thousands	Good	Fine	V. Fine
1803	98	16.00	32.00	50.00
1804 Stemless Wreath, All Kinds	1055	15.00	30.00	50.00
1804 Stems to Wreath	—	15.00	30.00	50.00
1805 Small 5, Stemless Wreath, All Kinds	814	20.00	40.00	50.00
1805 Small 5, Stems	—	65.00	225.00	650.00
1805 Stems to Wreath, Large 5	—	15.00	30.00	50.00
1806 Stemless, All Kinds	356	15.00	30.00	50.00
1806 Stems, Small 6	—	35.00	125.00	225.00
1806 Stems, Large 6	—	15.00	25.00	40.00
1807	476	15.00	30.00	55.00
1808 over 7, All Kinds	400	50.00	125.00	250.00
1808	—	16.00	30.00	50.00

TURBAN HEAD TYPE

	Mintage in Thousands	Good	Fine	V. Fine
1809 over 6, All Kinds	1155	15.00	30.00	55.00
1809	—	15.00	30.00	50.00
1810	215	20.00	45.00	70.00
1811	63	50.00	135.00	225.00

	Mintage in Thousands	Good	Fine	V. Fine	Unc.
1825	63	15.00	25.00	35.00	550.00
1826	234	15.00	22.50	32.50	500.00
1828 13 Stars, All Kinds	606	15.00	20.00	30.00	500.00
1828 12 Stars	—	18.00	35.00	60.00	650.00
1829	487	16.00	24.00	33.00	500.00

	Mintage in Thousands	Good	Fine	V. Fine	Unc.	Proof
1831	2	—	—	—	—	2,500.00
1832	154	15.00	22.50	35.00	250.00	1,250.00
1833	120	15.00	22.00	35.00	250.00	1,000.00
1834	141	15.00	22.50	35.00	250.00	1,000.00
1835	398	15.00	22.50	35.00	250.00	1,000.00
1836 Original	—	—	—	—	—	2,500.00
1836 Restrike	—	—	—	—	—	1,800.00

	Mintage in Thousands	Good	Fine	V. Fine	Unc.	Proof
1840-1849 Small Date, Proof only, each—1,500.00						
1849 Large Date ..	40	17.50	30.00	45.00	300.00	—
1850...................	40	17.50	30.00	40.00	300.00	—
1851:...................	148	16.00	25.00	30.00	250.00	—
1852 Proof only ...	—	—	—	—	—	1,500.00
1853........:..........	130	16.00	25.00	30.00	250.00	—
1854...................	55	16.00	25.00	30.00	250.00	900.00

	Mintage in Thousands	Good	Fine	V. Fine	Unc.	Proof
1855...................	57	16.00	25.00	30.00	250.00	900.00
1856...................	40	16.00	25.00	30.00	250.00	900.00
1857...................	35	25.00	35.00	55.00	300.00	1,100.00

Note: The value for Unc. and Proof is for M.S.-60 (i.e. "Mint State-60") condition. This grade shows absolutely no wear, but may be toned, have bag or keg marks, or have an uneven strike.

The value for the ultimate grade of M.S.-65 (i.e. "Mint State-65") would be, typically, three to five times that of M.S.-60. Characteristics of "M.S.-65" are: absolutely full mint color, perfectly flawless surfaces, and an exceptional strike. This divergence in values between M.S.-60 and M.S.-65 specimens hold approximately true for just about every 19th century issue; the gap between M.S.-60 and M.S.-65 for most 20th century issues is even wider.

25.

ONE-CENT PIECES—
1793–1857

Note: All large cents in *fair* to *about good* condition (i.e. unmutilated but worn) are valued at about one-third of the good column.

CHAIN TYPE

	Mintage in Thousands	Good	Fine	V. Fine	—
1793 Chain type, AMERI	636	2,000.00	3,000.00	6,500.00	—
1793 Chain type, AMERICA	—	1,500.00	2,500.00	5,500.00	—

WREATH TYPE

	Mintage in Thousands	Good	Fine	V. Fine	
1793 Wreath Type, Vine and Bars on Edge, All Kinds	63	1,000.00	1,600.00	3,000.00	—
1793 Wreath type, Lettered Edge.............	—	1,000.00	1,650.00	3,200.00	—

LIBERTY CAP TYPE

	Mintage in Thousands	Good	Fine	V. Fine	—
1793 Liberty Cap type	11	1,100.00	2,000.00	4,000.00	—
1794, All Kinds	919	90.00	150.00	325.00	—
1794 Starred Rev.	—	750.00	2,300.00	4,000.00	—
1795 Lettered Edge	37	80.00	175.00	350.00	—
1795 Plain Edge	502	75.00	150.00	275.00	—
1796 Liberty Cap type	110	90.00	175.00	375.00	—

DRAPED BUST TYPE

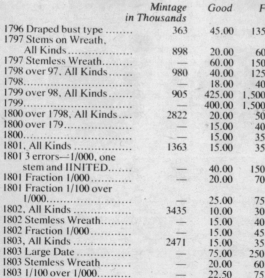

	Mintage in Thousands	Good	Fine	V. Fine	—
1796 Draped bust type	363	45.00	135.00	275.00	—
1797 Stems on Wreath, All Kinds	898	20.00	60.00	125.00	—
1797 Stemless Wreath	—	60.00	150.00	300.00	—
1798 over 97, All Kinds	980	40.00	125.00	240.00	—
1798	—	18.00	40.00	100.00	—
1799 over 98, All Kinds	905	425.00	1,500.00	3,000.00	—
1799	—	400.00	1,500.00	2,850.00	—
1800 over 1798, All Kinds	2822	20.00	50.00	100.00	—
1800 over 179	—	15.00	40.00	90.00	—
1800	—	15.00	35.00	80.00	—
1801, All Kinds	1363	15.00	35.00	80.00	—
1801 3 errors—1/000, one stem and IINITED	—	40.00	150.00	325.00	—
1801 Fraction 1/000	—	20.00	70.00	150.00	—
1801 Fraction 1/100 over 1/000	—	25.00	75.00	150.00	—
1802, All Kinds	3435	10.00	30.00	70.00	—
1802 Stemless Wreath	—	15.00	40.00	80.00	—
1802 Fraction 1/000	—	15.00	45.00	90.00	—
1803, All Kinds	2471	15.00	35.00	70.00	—
1803 Large Date	—	75.00	250.00	550.00	—
1803 Stemless Wreath	—	20.00	60.00	120.00	—
1803 1/100 over 1/000	—	22.50	75.00	160.00	—

	Mintage in Thousands	Good	Fine	V. Fine	—
1804	757	250.00	625.00	1,100.00	—
1805	941	15.00	35.00	75.00	—
1806	348	25.00	75.00	175.00	—
1807 over 6, Large 7, All Kinds	727	15.00	35.00	75.00	—
1807 Over 6, Small 7	—	75.00	225.00	400.00	—
1807	—	15.00	35.00	75.00	—

TURBAN HEAD TYPE

	Mintage in Thousands	Good	Fine	V. Fine	—
1808 13 Stars, All Kinds	1109	20.00	75.00	145.00	—
1808 12 Stars	—	20.00	75.00	160.00	—
1809	223	75.00	200.00	375.00	—
1810 over 9, All Kinds	1459	17.50	50.00	140.00	—
1810	—	15.00	40.00	135.00	—
1811 over 10, All Kinds	218	60.00	150.00	250.00	—
1811	—	60.00	150.00	265.00	—
1812	1076	15.00	40.00	135.00	—
1813	418	30.00	80.00	150.00	—
1814	358	15.00	40.00	135.00	—

CORONET TYPE

	Mintage in Thousands	Good	Fine	V. Fine	Unc.
1816	2821	7.50	15.00	30.00	275.00
1817, All Kinds	3948	7.50	15.00	25.00	240.00
1817 15 Stars	—	9.00	30.00	50.00	650.00
1818	3167	7.50	15.00	25.00	235.00
1819 over 18, All Kinds	2671	8.50	20.00	30.00	400.00
1819	—	7.50	15.00	25.00	250.00
1820 over 19, All Kinds	4408	8.50	17.00	30.00	300.00
1820	—	6.50	13.00	22.50	245.00
1821	389	17.50	40.00	80.00	1,150.00
1822	2072	7.00	15.00	30.00	350.00
1823 over 22, All Kinds	856	25.00	65.00	150.00	2,500.00

	Mintage in Thousands	Good	Fine	V. Fine	Unc.
1823	—	35.00	90.00	200.00	3,000.00
1824 over 22, All Kinds	1262	15.00	35.00	70.00	—
1824	—	7.50	20.00	35.00	650.00
1825	1461	7.50	18.00	30.00	425.00
1826	1517	7.50	18.00	30.00	325.00
1827	2358	6.50	15.00	30.00	275.00
1828	2261	6.50	15.00	30.00	400.00
1829	1415	6.50	15.00	30.00	350.00
1830	1712	6.50	15.00	30.00	325.00
1831	3359	6.50	15.00	30.00	325.00
1832	2362	6.50	15.00	30.00	325.00
1833	2739	6.50	15.00	30.00	300.00
1834	1855	6.50	15.00	30.00	325.00
1835 Type of '34, All Kinds	3878	8.50	25.00	40.00	350.00
1835 Type of '36	—	6.50	15.00	30.00	325.00
1836	2111	6.50	15.00	20.00	275.00
1837 Plain Hair Cord, All Kinds	5558	6.50	20.00	27.00	290.00
1837 Beaded Hair Cord	—	6.50	16.00	22.00	275.00
1838	6370	6.50	12.00	20.00	235.00
1839 over 36 Line under CENT, No dot, All Kinds	3129	100.00	250.00	400.00	—
1839 Type of '38, Line under cent	—	10.00	20.00	40.00	350.00
1839 Silly Head, Line under CENT; No center dot	—	10.00	25.00	40.00	400.00
1839 Booby Head, no line under CENT	—	10.00	20.00	35.00	500.00
1839 Type of '40, no line under CENT	—	10.00	30.00	40.00	450.00

BRAIDED HAIR TYPE

	Mintage in Thousands	Good	Fine	V. Fine	Unc.
1840	2463	6.50	15.00	20.00	250.00
1841	1597	6.50	15.00	20.00	250.00
1842	2383	6.50	15.00	20.00	250.00
1843 Obverse and Reverse of 1842, All Kinds	2428	6.50	20.00	35.00	250.00
1843 Obverse of 1842, Reverse of '44	—	20.00	60.00	90.00	800.00
1843 Obverse and Reverse of 1844		8.00	15.00	30.00	300.00
1844, All Kinds	2399	6.50	12.00	18.00	250.00
1844/81	—	10.00	16.00	40.00	400.00
1845	3895	6.00	9.00	12.00	250.00

	Mintage in Thousands	Good	Fine	V. Fine	Unc.
1846	4121	6.00	9.00	12.00	250.00
1847	6184	6.00	9.00	12.00	250.00
1848	6416	6.00	9.00	12.00	250.00
1849	4179	6.00	9.00	12.00	250.00
1850	4427	6.00	9.00	12.00	250.00
1851	9890	6.00	9.00	12.00	250.00
1851/81	—	10.00	20.00	50.00	375.00
1852	5063	6.00	9.00	12.00	250.00
1853	6641	6.00	9.00	12.00	250.00
1854	4236	6.00	9.00	12.00	250.00
1855	1575	6.00	9.00	12.00	250.00
1856	2690	6.00	9.00	12.00	250.00
1857	333	30.00	40.00	50.00	400.00

FLYING EAGLE CENTS—1856-1858

COPPER-NICKEL ("WHITE" CENTS)

	Mintage in Thousands	Good	Fine	V. Fine	Unc.	Proof
1856	1	800.00	1,250.00	1,400.00	2,500.00	3,000.00
1857	17,450	7.50	11.00	25.00	400.00	2,750.00
1858 Large Letters, All Kinds	24,600	7.50	12.00	25.00	450.00	2,600.00
1858 Small Letters	—	7.50	12.00	25.00	425.00	2,600.00

INDIAN HEAD CENTS—1859-1864

COPPER-NICKEL OR "WHITE"

1859   1860–1864

1859	36,400	3.50	8.50	16.00	450.00	1,000.00
1860	20,566	3.25	7.00	11.50	250.00	675.00
1861	10,100	6.00	14.00	18.00	300.00	750.00
1862	28,075	3.00	5.00	13.00	200.00	600.00
1863	49,840	3.00	5.00	7.50	200.00	600.00
1864	13,740	4.50	11.00	16.00	250.00	750.00

1864-1909 BRONZE

	Mintage in Thousands	Good	Fine	V. Fine	Unc.	Proof
1864 No L Bronze, All Kinds.....	39,234	2.50	6.50	12.50	65.00	800.00
1864 L on ribbon .	—	12.00	45.00	60.00	250.00	—
1865..................	35,429	2.00	6.00	10.00	50.00	300.00
1866..................	9827	10.00	25.00	40.00	150.00	300.00
1867..................	9821	10.00	25.00	40.00	150.00	325.00
1868..................	10,267	10.00	25.00	40.00	150.00	300.00
1869 over 8, All Kinds.....	6420	42.00	125.00	200.00	800.00	—
1869..................	—	15.00	50.00	75.00	300.00	450.00
1870..................	5275	14.00	40.00	60.00	200.00	300.00
1871..................	3930	16.00	47.00	70.00	225.00	400.00
1872..................	4042	20.00	55.00	90.00	325.00	450.00
1873..................	11,677	4.00	12.00	20.00	90.00	250.00
1874..................	14,188	4.00	12.00	20.00	90.00	240.00
1875..................	13,528	4.00	12.00	20.00	90.00	230.00
1876..................	7944	7.00	18.00	30.00	110.00	200.00
1877..................	853	100.00	190.00	275.00	1,500.00	1,800.00
1878..................	5800	6.00	25.00	42.00	125.00	160.00
1879..................	16,231	1.50	5.00	10.00	45.00	125.00
1880..................	38,965	.75	3.00	5.00	30.00	110.00
1881..................	39,212	.75	3.00	5.00	30.00	110.00
1882..................	38,581	.75	3.00	5.00	30.00	110.00
1883..................	45,598	.75	3.00	5.00	30.00	110.00
1884..................	23,262	1.50	4.00	8.00	40.00	110.00
1885..................	11,265	3.00	10.00	15.00	50.00	140.00
1886..................	17,654	1.75	5.00	10.00	40.00	130.00
1887..................	45,226	.80	1.75	3.00	30.00	100.00
1888..................	37,494	.80	1.75	3.00	30.00	100.00
1889..................	48,869	.80	1.75	3.00	30.00	100.00
1890..................	57,183	.80	1.75	3.00	30.00	100.00
1891..................	47,072	.80	1.75	3.00	30.00	100.00
1892..................	37,650	.80	1.75	3.00	30.00	100.00
1893..................	46,642	.80	1.75	3.00	30.00	100.00
1894..................	16,752	1.50	6.00	10.00	50.00	125.00
1895..................	38,344	.75	1.50	3.00	30.00	100.00
1896..................	39,057	.75	1.50	3.00	30.00	100.00
1897..................	50,466	.75	1.50	3.00	30.00	100.00
1898..................	49,823	.75	1.50	3.00	30.00	100.00
1899..................	53,600	.75	1.00	1.50	30.00	100.00
1900..................	66,834	.75	1.00	1.50	30.00	100.00
1901..................	79,611	.75	1.00	1.50	30.00	100.00
1902..................	87,377	.75	1.00	1.50	30.00	100.00
1903..................	85,094	.75	1.00	1.50	30.00	100.00
1904..................	61,328	.75	1.00	1.50	30.00	100.00
1905..................	80,719	.75	1.00	1.50	30.00	100.00

	Mintage in Thousands	Good	Fine	V. Fine	Unc.	Proof
1906	96,022	.70	.75	1.50	30.00	100.00
1907	108,139	.70	.75	1.50	30.00	110.00
1908	32,328	.70	.75	1.50	30.00	115.00
1908S	1115	18.00	25.00	30.00	120.00	—
1909	14,371	.90	1.50	3.00	38.00	125.00
1909S	309	65.00	85.00	100.00	275.00	—

LINCOLN HEAD CENTS—1909-Date

1909–1958   1959–1964

	Mintage in Thousands	Good	Fine	Ex. Fine	Unc.	Proof
1909 V D B	27,995	1.25	1.75	3.00	9.00	550.00
1909S, V D B	484	250.00	325.00	425.00	625.00	—
1909	72,703	.30	.40	1.00	9.00	90.00
1909S	1825	35.00	40.00	55.00	125.00	—
1910	146,801	.15	.30	1.50	9.00	85.00
1910S	6045	5.00	7.50	10.00	70.00	—
1911	101,178	.15	.60	3.00	11.00	95.00
1911D	12,672	2.50	5.00	14.00	70.00	—
1911S	4026	9.00	11.00	18.00	80.00	—
1912	68,153	.20	1.50	5.50	18.00	90.00
1912D	10,411	2.25	5.00	17.50	70.00	—
1912S	4431	7.00	12.00	20.00	70.00	—
1913	76,532	.15	1.00	6.00	18.00	85.00
1913D	15,804	1.25	3.00	14.00	60.00	—
1913S	6101	4.00	6.50	14.00	70.00	—
1914	75,238	.15	1.50	6.00	30.00	200.00
1914D	1193	60.00	85.00	250.00	800.00	—
1914S	4137	6.00	8.00	17.00	110.00	—
1915	29,092	.60	4.00	18.00	70.00	250.00
1915D	22,050	.50	1.50	7.00	35.00	—
1915S	4833	5.00	6.00	14.00	70.00	—
1916	131,834	.15	.35	2.00	10.00	275.00
1916D	35,956	.20	.75	5.00	25.00	—
1916S	22,510	.50	1.00	5.00	35.00	—
1917	196,430	.15	.30	2.00	10.00	—
1917D	55,120	.20	.60	5.00	30.00	—
1917S	32,620	.20	.60	5.00	30.00	—
1918	298,103	.15	.30	2.00	11.00	—
1918D	47,830	.20	.60	5.00	35.00	—
1918S	34,680	.20	.50	4.00	35.00	—
1919	392,021	.15	.30	1.00	9.00	—
1919D	57,154	.20	.50	1.25	25.00	—
1919S	139,760	.20	.40	2.00	20.00	—
1920	310,165	.15	.30	1.25	9.00	—
1920D	49,280	.15	.45	3.00	30.00	—
1920S	46,220	.15	.45	3.00	30.00	—
1921	39,157	.15	.50	3.00	25.00	—

	Mintage in Thousands	Good	Fine	Ex. Fine	Unc.	
1921S	15,274	.50	1.00	9.00	175.00	—
1922D, All Kinds	7,160	5.00	7.00	15.00	65.00	—
1922 No "D"	—	150.00	250.00	500.00	2,500.00	—

	Mintage in Thousands	Good	Fine	Ex. Fine	Unc.	Proof
1923	74,723	.15	.30	1.25	9.00	
1923S	8,700	1.25	1.50	15.00	150.00	
1924	75,178	.15	.30	1.25	17.00	
1924D	2,520	8.00	10.00	30.00	195.00	
1924S	11,696	.50	.80	4.00	125.00	
1925	139,949	.15	.25	1.00	8.00	
1925D	22,580	.20	.50	4.00	40.00	
1925S	26,380	.20	.50	4.00	35.00	
1926	157,088	.15	.30	1.00	7.00	
1926D	28,020	.20	.50	2.00	30.00	
1926S	4,550	3.00	4.00	16.00	100.00	
1927	144,440	.15	.30	1.00	7.00	
1927D	27,170	.20	.50	1.25	25.00	
1927S	14,276	.30	.75	4.00	50.00	
1928	134,116	.15	.30	4.00	7.00	
1928D	31,170	.15	.30	1.00	20.00	
1928S	17,266	.25	.60	2.00	35.00	
1929	185,262	.15	.30	.50	6.00	
1929D	41,730	.15	.30	.80	9.00	
1929S	50,148	.15	.30	.80	7.00	
1930	157,415	.15	.30	.80	4.00	
1930D	40,100	.15	.30	.80	7.00	
1930S	24,286	.15	.30	.80	7.00	
1931	19,396	.25	.40	1.00	15.00	
1931D	4,480	2.50	3.50	7.00	40.00	
1931S	866	30.00	35.00	40.00	60.00	
1932	9,062	1.00	15.00	2.50	15.00	
1932D	10,500	.40	.60	1.00	11.00	
1933	14,360	.40	.50	1.50	15.00	
1933D	6,200	1.25	2.00	3.00	18.00	
1934	219,080	—	—	—	2.00	
1934D	28,446	—	—	1.00	12.00	
1935	345,388	—	—	—	1.00	
1935D	47,000	—	—	—	1.25	
1935S	38,702	—	—	—	4.00	400.00
1936	309,638	—	—	—	1.00	
1936D	40,620	—	—	—	1.25	
1936S	29,130	—	—	—	1.50	
1937	309,179	—	—	—	1.00	200.00
1937D	56,430	—	—	—	1.40	
1937S	34,500	—	—	—	1.00	
1938	157,697	—	—	—	1.00	100.00
1938D	20,010	—	—	—	2.25	
1938S	15,180	—	—	.60	3.00	
1939	316,480	—	—	—	.75	65.00
1939D	15,160	—	—	.65	3.00	
1939S	52,079	—	—	—	1.25	
1940	586,826	—	—	—	.60	50.00
1940D	81,390	—	—	—	1.00	
1940S	112,940	—	—	—	.80	

	Mintage in Thousands	Unc.	Proof
1941	887,039	.60	50.00
1941D	128,700	1.75	
1941S	92,360	4.50	
1942	657,827	.40	50.00
1942D	206,688	.40	
1942S	85,590	3.00	
1943 Steel	684,629	1.00	
1943D Steel	217,660	2.00	
1943S Steel	191,550	2.50	
1944 Copper	1,435,400	.40	
1944D	430,578	.30	
1944S	282,760	.40	
1945	1,040,515	.35	
1945D	226,268	.40	
1945S	181,770	.50	
1946	991,655	.25	
1946D	315,690	.30	
1946S	198,100	.60	
1947	190,555	.50	
1947D	194,750	.60	
1947S	99,000	.65	
1948	317,570	.40	
1948D	172,638	.40	
1948S	81,735	.50	
1949	217,775	.65	
1949D	153,133	.65	
1949S	64,290	1.00	
1950	272,686	.40	80.00
1950D	334,950	.40	
1950S	118,550	.75	
1951	284,634	1.00	35.00
1951D	625,355	.30	
1951S	136,010	1.00	
1952	186,857	.55	30.00
1952D	746,130	.35	
1952S	137,800	.60	
1953	256,884	.35	25.00
1953D	700,515	.35	
1953S	181,835	.50	
1954	71,873	.60	10.00
1954D	251,553	.30	
1954S	96,190	.40	
1955	330,958	.25	10.00

	Mintage in Thousands	Fine	Ex. Fine	Unc.	Proof
1955 Double Die Obverse	—	250.00	350.00	500.00	
1955D	563,258	—	—	.20	
1955S	44,610	—	—	.75	
1956	421,414	—	—	.15	3.00
1956D	1,098,201	—	—	.10	
1957	283,788	—	—	.10	2.00
1957D	1,051,342	—	—	.10	
1958	253,401	—	—	.15	2.00
1958D	800,953	—	—	:10	

MEMORIAL REVERSE TYPE

	Mintage in Thousands	Fine	Ex. Fine	Unc.	Proof
1959	610,864	—	—	.10	1.00

	Mintage in Thousands	Fine	Ex. Fine	Unc.	Proof
1959D	1,279,760	—	—	.10	
1960 Large Date, All Kinds	588,097	—	—	.10	1.00
1960 Small Date	—	2.00	3.00	5.00	20.00
1960D Large Date, All Kinds	1,580,884	—	—	.10	
1960D Small Date	—	—	—	.50	
1961	756,373	—	—	.05	.50
1961D	1,753,267	—	—	.05	
1962	609,263	—	—	.05	.50
1962D	1,793,148	—	—	.05	
1963	757,186	—	—	.05	.50
1963D	1,774,020	—	—	.05	
1964	2,652,526	—	—	.05	.50
1964D	3,799,072	—	—	.05	
1965	1,497,225	—	—	.05	
1966	2,188,148	—	—	.05	
1967	3,048,667	—	—	.05	
1968	1,707,881	—	—	.05	
1968D	2,886,270	—	—	.05	
1968S	261,312	—	—	.05	.50
1969	1,136,910	—	—	.25	
1969D	4,002,832	—	—	.05	
1969S	547,310	—	—	.10	.50
1970	1,898,315	—	—	.05	
1970D	2,891,439	—	—	.05	
1970S	693,193	—	—	.05	.50
1971	1,919,490	—	—	.05	
1971D	2,911,046	—	—	.05	
1971S	528,354	—	—	.05	.50
1972	2,933,255	—	—	.05	
1972 Double Die Obv	—	75.00	125.00	225.00	
1972D	2,665,071	—	—	.05	
1972S	380,200	—	—	.05	.50
1973	3,728,245	—	—	.05	
1973D	3,549,577	—	—	.05	
1973S	3,191,938	—	—	.05	.50
1974	4,232,141	—	—	.05	
1974D	4,335,098	—	—	.05	
1974S	412,039	—	—	.05	.50
1975	5,451,476	—	—	.05	
1975D	4,505,245	—	—	.05	
1975S Proof only	2,909	—	—	12.00	
1976 P&D	8,895,885	—	—	.05	
1976S Proof only	4,150	—	—	6.50	
1977 P&D	8,663,992	—	—	.05	
1977S Proof only	3,251	—	—	4.00	
1978 P&D	9,838,838	—	—	.05	
1978S Proof only	3,128	—	—	3.50	
1979 P&D	10,157,872	—	—	.05	
1979S Proof only	3,677	—	—	—	2.50
1980 P&D	—	—	—	.05	
1980S Proof only	—	—	—	—	2.00
1981 P&D	—	—	—	.05	
1981S Proof only	—	—	—	—	2.00

26.
BRONZE TWO-CENT PIECES—
1864–1873

	Mintage in Thousands	Good	Fine	Unc.	Proof
1864 Small Motto, All Kinds	19,848	40.00	70.00	500.00	—
1864 Large Motto	—	5.00	8.00	175.00	375.00
1865................................	13,640	5.00	8.00	175.00	375.00
1866................................	3177	5.00	8.00	175.00	375.00
1867................................	2939	5.00	8.00	175.00	375.00
1868................................	2804	5.00	8.00	175.00	375.00
1869................................	1547	5.00	8.00	200.00	375.00
1869 Over 8	—	75.00	100.00	650.00	—
1870................................	861	6.00	12.00	210.00	400.00
1871................................	721	8.00	15.00	240.00	450.00
1872................................	65	40.00	60.00	400.00	650.00
1873................................	1	—	—	—	1,100.00

Note: Uncirculated two-cent pieces with full, original ''mint red'' color sell at a premium price.

27.

NICKEL THREE-CENT PIECES—
1865–1889

	Mintage in Thousands	Good	Fine	Unc.	Proof
1865	11,382	5.00	7.00	150.00	1,200.00
1866	4801	5.00	7.00	150.00	500.00
1867	3915	5.00	7.00	150.00	500.00
1868	3252	5.00	7.00	150.00	500.00
1869	1604	5.00	7.00	150.00	500.00
1870	1335	5.00	7.00	150.00	500.00
1871	604	6.00	8.00	150.00	500.00
1872	862	6.00	8.00	150.00	500.00
1873	1173	5.00	7.00	150.00	500.00
1874	790	5.00	7.00	150.00	500.00
1875	228	7.00	11.00	180.00	500.00
1876	162	8.00	11.00	180.00	500.00
1877	1	—	—	—	1,000.00
1878	2	—	—	—	700.00
1879	41	30.00	50.00	300.00	550.00
1880	25	30.00	55.00	300.00	550.00
1881	1681	5.00	7.00	150.00	550.00
1882	25	35.00	60.00	400.00	550.00
1883	11	45.00	70.00	400.00	550.00
1884	6	60.00	90.00	400.00	550.00
1885	5	80.00	110.00	400.00	550.00
1886	4	—	—	—	550.00
1887 7 over 6, All Kinds	8	—	—	—	550.00
1887	—	70.00	100.00	400.00	550.00
1888	41	35.00	55.00	400.00	550.00
1889	22	35.00	55.00	400.00	550.00

28.

NICKEL FIVE-CENT PIECES—
1866–1883

SHIELD TYPE

1866–1867   1867–1883

	Mintage in Thousands	Good	Fine	Unc.	Proof
1866	14,743	8.00	17.00	500.00	1,750.00
1867 Rays	2019	10.00	25.00	350.00	3,500.00
1867 Without Rays	28,891	7.00	12.00	200.00	750.00
1868	28,817	7.00	12.00	200.00	750.00
1869	16,395	7.00	14.00	200.00	750.00
1870	4806	8.00	16.00	200.00	750.00
1871	561	40.00	60.00	300.00	1,000.00
1872	6036	7.00	14.00	200.00	750.00
1873	4550	7.00	14.00	200.00	750.00
1874	3538	10.00	20.00	200.00	750.00
1875	2097	15.00	30.00	250.00	750.00
1876	2530	10.00	20.00	200.00	750.00
1877	1	—	—	—	1,800.00
1878	2	—	—	—	900.00
1879	29	150.00	200.00	500.00	750.00
1880	20	180.00	250.00	550.00	750.00
1881	72	140.00	200.00	500.00	750.00
1882	11,476	7.00	14.00	200.00	750.00
1883	1457	7.00	14.00	200.00	750.00
1883 over 2	—	15.00	35.00	350.00	750.00

Note: Choice, well struck uncirculated shield nickels, especially 1866-74, are worth more than the listed prices.

LIBERTY HEAD TYPE

1883

1883–1912

	Mintage in Thousands	Good	Fine	Unc.	Proof
1883 Without CENTS.........	5480	2.00	4.00	40.00	300.00
1883 With CENTS	16,033	5.00	10.00	200.00	250.00
1884................................	11,274	5.00	10.00	220.00	250.00
1885................................	1476	200.00	300.00	900.00	900.00
1886................................	3330	30.00	60.00	400.00	500.00
1887................................	15,264	3.00	8.00	175.00	250.00
1888................................	10,720	6.00	10.00	175.00	250.00
1889................................	15,881	3.50	8.00	175.00	250.00
1890................................	16,259	4.00	10.00	175.00	250.00
1891................................	16,834	3.00	8.00	175.00	250.00
1892................................	11,700	3.00	8.00	175.00	250.00
1893................................	13,370	3.00	8.00	175.00	250.00
1894................................	5413	5.00	12.00	175.00	250.00
1895................................	9980	2.00	8.00	175.00	250.00
1896................................	8843	2.00	12.00	175.00	250.00
1897................................	20,429	1.00	8.00	175.00	250.00
1898................................	12,532	1.00	8.00	175.00	250.00
1899................................	26,029	1.00	8.00	175.00	250.00
1900................................	27,256	.50	2.50	175.00	250.00
1901................................	26,480	.50	2.50	175.00	250.00
1902................................	31,490	.50	2.50	175.00	250.00
1903................................	28,007	.50	2.50	175.00	250.00
1904................................	21,405	.50	2.50	175.00	250.00
1905................................	29,827	.50	2.50	175.00	250.00
1906................................	38,614	.50	2.50	175.00	250.00
1907................................	39,215	.50	2.50	175.00	250.00
1908................................	22,686	.50	2.50	175.00	250.00
1909................................	11,591	.50	2.50	175.00	250.00
1910................................	30,169	.50	2.50	175.00	250.00
1911................................	39,559	.50	2.50	175.	250.00
1912................................	26,237	.50	2.50	175.00	250.00
1912D	8474	1.50	7.00	250.00	—
1912S................................	238	30.00	50.00	500.00	—
1913 Liberty Head	(5 struck)	—	Rare	—	—

INDIAN HEAD OR BUFFALO TYPE

1913

1913–1938

	Mintage in Thousands	Good	Fine	Unc.	Matte Proof
1913 Var. 1	30,994	1.50	3.00	50.00	500.00
1913D Var. 1	5337	4.00	6.00	70.00	—
1913S Var. 1	2105	7.00	12.00	125.00	—
1913 Var. 2	29,859	2.50	3.50	50.00	500.00
1913D Var. 2	4156	30.00	40.00	200.00	—
1913S Var. 2	1209	55.00	80.00	300.00	—
1914	20,666	3.00	5.00	60.00	500.00
1914D	3912	20.00	30.00	250.00	—
1914S	3420	4.00	8.50	135.00	—
1915	20,987	1.25	3.00	60.00	500.00
1915D	7570	4.00	10.00	140.00	—
1915S	1505	7.00	15.00	275.00	—
1916	63,498	.50	1.50	40.00	600.00
1916D	13,333	3.50	6.50	160.00	—
1916S	11,860	2.00	5.50	160.00	—
1917	51,224	.60	1.50	45.00	—
1917D	9911	3.50	8.50	240.00	—
1917S	4193	2.75	9.00	270.00	—
1918	32,086	.50	2.00	90.00	—
1918D over 7, All Kinds	8362	400.00	700.00	10,000.00	—
1918D Normal date	—	2.75	8.50	350.00	—
1918S	4882	2.00	8.50	310.00	—
1919	60,868	.40	1.25	40.00	—
1919D	8006	2.75	10.00	400.00	—
1919S	7521	2.00	8.00	330.00	—
1920	63,093	.40	1.00	40.00	—
1920D	9418	2.50	8.00	350.00	—
1920S	9689	1.25	6.00	275.00	—
1921	10,663	.75	3.00	95.00	—
1921S	1557	8.00	28.00	500.00	—
1923	35,715	.40	1.00	45.00	—
1923S	6142	1.50	6.00	200.00	—
1924	21,620	.40	1.00	55.00	—
1924D	5258	2.00	8.00	250.00	—
1924S	1437	4.00	15.00	750.00	—
1925	35,565	.40	1.00	40.00	—
1925D	4450	3.00	7.00	325.00	—
1925S	6256	2.00	6.00	250.00	—

	Mintage in Thousands	Good	Fine	Unc.
1926	44,693	.40	1.00	35.00
1926D	5,638	1.75	8.00	190.00
1926S	970	5.00	13.00	600.00
1927	37,981	.40	1.00	35.00
1927D	5,730	.60	2.75	115.00
1927S	3,430	1.00	4.00	275.00
1928	23,411	.35	.75	35.00
1928D	6,436	.50	1.50	50.00
1928S	6,936	.60	1.50	85.00
1929	36,446	.30	.60	30.00
1929D	8,370	.45	1.00	60.00
1929S	7,754	.45	.95	45.00
1930	22,849	.35	.75	40.00
1930S	5,435	.60	1.50	60.00
1931S	1,200	3.50	5.50	60.00
1934	20,213	.30	.60	40.00
1934D	7,480	.40	.70	80.00
1935	58,264	.30	.50	22.50
1935D	12,092	.30	.50	80.00
1935S	10,300	.30	.50	35.00
1936 (Proof $1,000)	119,001	.30	.50	22.50
1936D	24,814	.30	.50	23.50
1936S	14,930	.30	.50	29.00
1937 (Proof $750)	79,486	.30	.50	20.00
1937D, All Kinds	17,826	.30	.50	21.00
1937D, 3-Legged Var	—	135.00	185.00	675.00
1937S	5,635	.30	.50	22.50
1938D, All Kinds	7,020	.30	.50	20.00
1938D/S	—	3.00	5.00	30.00

JEFFERSON TYPE

	Mintage in Thousands	—	Ex. Fine	Unc.	Proof
1938	19,515	—	.45	2.50	60.00
1938D	5376	—	1.85	10.00	—
1938S	4105	—	3.00	11.00	50.00
1939	120,628	—	.35	1.00	—
1939D	3514	—	7.50	60.00	—
1939S	6630	—	2.50	40.00	—
1940	176,499	—	—	1.00	40.00
1940D	43,540	—	—	2.00	—
1940S	39,690	—	—	2.00	—
1941	203,284	—	—	.80	40.00
1941D	53,432	—	—	2.50	—
1941S	43,445	—	—	3.00	—
1942	49,819	—	—	1.75	40.00
1942D	13,938	—	1.75	30.00	—

	Mintage in Thousands	—	Ex. Fine	Unc.	Proof
1942P Wartime Silver Nickels	57,901	—	1.50	20.00	100.00
1942S	32,900	—	1.00	16.00	—
1943P	271,165	—	.75	5.00	—
1943D	15,294	—	2.10	5.00	—
1943S	104,060	—	.75	8.00	—
1944P	119,150	—	.75	5.00	—
1944D	32,309	—	.85	6.00	—
1944S	21,640	—	.95	8.00	—
1945P	119,408	—	.75	7.00	—
1945D	37,158	—	.75	6.00	—
1945S	58,939	—	.60	5.00	—
1946 Regular Nickels	161,116	—	—	.50	—
1946D	45,292	—	—	.65	—
1946S	13,560	—	—	1.00	—
1947	95,000	—	—	.35	—
1947D	37,822	—	—	.90	—
1947S	24,720	—	—	.80	—
1948	89,348	—	—	.40	—
1948D	44,734	—	—	.90	—
1948S	11,300	—	—	1.00	—
1949	60,652	—	—	1.00	—
1949D	36,498	—	—	1.00	—
1949S	9716	—	—	2.00	—
1950	9847	—	—	1.50	95.00
1950D	2630	6.50	7.50	9.50	—

	Mintage in Thousands	Unc.	Proof
1951	28,610	1.00	65.00
1951D	20,460	1.00	—
1951S	7776	3.00	—
1952	64,070	.50	40.00
1952D	30,638	1.50	—
1952S	20,572	.80	—
1953	46,773	.35	30.00
1953D	59,873	.50	—
1953S	19,211	.60	—
1954	47,914	.20	15.00
1954D	117,183	.20	—
1954S	29,384	.30	—
1955	8266	.90	10.00
1955D	74,464	.20	—
1956	35,885	.20	4.00
1956D	67,223	.20	—
1957	39,656	.20	2.00
1957D	136,829	.20	—
1958	17,964	.35	2.00
1958D	168,249	.15	—
1959	28,397	.20	2.00
1959D	160,738	.15	—
1960	57,108	.15	1.00
1960D	192,582	.15	—
1961	76,668	.15	1.00
1961D	229,343	.15	—
1962	100,602	.15	1.00
1962D	280,196	.15	—
1963	178,852	.15	1.00
1963D	276,829	.15	—

	Mintage in Thousands	Unc.	Proof
1964	1,028,623	.15	1.00
1964D	1,787,297	.15	—
1965	136,131	.15	—
1966	156,208	.15	—
1967	107,326	.15	—
1968D	91,228	.15	—
1968S	103,438	.15	.50
1969D	202,808	.15	—
1969S	123,100	.15	.50
1970D	515,485	.15	—
1970S	241,465	.15	.75
1971	106,884	.15	—
1971D	316,145	.15	—
1971S Proof only	3,224	—	1.50
1972	202,036	.15	—
1972D	351,695	.15	—
1972S Proof only	3,268	—	1.50
1973	384,396	.15	—
1973D	261,405	.15	—
1973S Proof only	2,770	—	2.25
1974	601,752	.15	—
1974D	277,373	.15	—
1974S Proof only	2,617	—	3.50
1975	181,772	.15	—
1975D	401,875	.15	—
1975S Proof only	2,909	—	1.50
1976 P-D	931,088	.15	—
1976S Proof only	4,150	—	.50
1977 P&D	882,689	.15	—
1977S Proof only	3,251		1.00
1978 P&D	704,402	.15	—
1978S Proof only	3,128		1.50
1979 P&D	819,056	.15	—
1979S Proof only	3,677		1.25
1980 P&D	—	.15	—
1980S Proof only	—		1.00
1981 P&D	—	.15	—
1981S Proof only	—	—	2.00

29.

SILVER THREE-CENT PIECES—
1851–1873

	Mintage in Thousands	Good	Fine	Unc.	Proof
1851	5447	7.00	15.00	350.00	—
1851O	720	12.00	30.00	400.00	—
1852	18,664	7.00	14.00	350.00	—
1853	11,400	7.00	14.00	350.00	—
1854	671	12.00	20.00	600.00	—
1855	139	18.00	30.00	800.00	2,500.00
1856	1458	14.00	25.00	600.00	1,900.00
1857	1042	14.00	25.00	600.00	1,850.00
1858	1604	14.00	25.00	600.00	1,500.00
1859	365	13.00	22.00	350.00	750.00
1860	287	13.00	22.00	350.00	750.00
1861	498	13.00	22.00	350.00	750.00
1862	344	13.00	22.00	350.00	750.00
1863	21	—	—	600.00	750.00
1864	12	—	—	650.00	750.00
1865	9	—	—	—	750.00
1866	23	—	—	—	750.00
1867	5	—	—	—	750.00
1868	4	—	—	—	750.00
1869	5	—	—	—	750.00
1870	4	—	—	—	750.00
1871	4	—	—	—	750.00
1872	2	—	—	—	750.00
1873	1	—	—	—	850.00

30.

HALF DIMES—
1794–1873

FLOWING HAIR TYPE

	Mintage in Thousands	Good	Fine	Unc.
1794, All Kinds	86	850.00	1,600.00	7,000.00
1795, All Kinds Total	—	800.00	1,500.00	6,000.00

DRAPED BUST TYPE

1796–1797   1800–1805

1796 over 5, All Kinds	10	750.00	1,600.00	7,500.00
1796 Normal Date	—	750.00	1,500.00	8,000.00
1796 LIKERTY	—	700.00	1,500.00	8,000.00
1797 15 Stars, All Kinds	45	700.00	1,500.00	7,500.00
1797 16 Stars	—	700.00	1,500.00	7,000.00
1797 13 Stars	—	700.00	1,500.00	7,500.00
1800, All Kinds	24	500.00	1,100.00	6,500.00
1800 LIBEKTY	—	500.00	1,100.00	6,500.00
1801	34	500.00	1,100.00	6,500.00
1802	13	3,000.00	6,000.00	6,500.00
1803	38	500.00	1,100.00	—
1805	16	650.00	1,750.00	—

LIBERTY CAP TYPE

	Mintage in Thousands	Good	Fine	Unc.
1829	1230	15.00	25.00	450.00
1830	1240	15.00	25.00	450.00
1831	1243	15.00	25.00	450.00
1832	965	15.00	25.00	450.00
1833	1370	15.00	25.00	450.00
1834	1480	15.00	25.00	450.00
1835	2760	15.00	25.00	450.00
1836	1900	15.00	25.00	450.00
1837	2276	15.00	25.00	450.00

LIBERTY SEATED TYPE

1837–1838   1838–1859   1860–1873

	Mintage in Thousands	Good	Fine	Unc.
1837 No Stars	(included above)	37.50	70.00	1,000.00
1838O No Stars	70	45.00	100.00	3,000.00
1838 No Drapery at Elbow	2255	5.00	10.00	700.00
1839 No Drapery at Elbow	1069	5.00	10.00	700.00
1839O No Drapery at Elbow	1034	7.50	15.00	750.00
1840 No Drapery at Elbow	1344	5.00	10.00	700.00
1840O No Drapery at Elbow, All Kinds	935	7.00	18.00	800.00
1840 Drapery at Elbow	—	4.50	8.00	400.00
1840O Drapery at Elbow	—	7.00	18.00	600.00
1841	1150	4.50	8.00	400.00
1841O	815	6.00	11.00	550.00
1842	815	4.50	8.00	400.00
1842O	350	8.00	20.00	800.00
1843	1165	4.50	8.00	400.00
1844	430	6.00	11.00	400.00
1844O	220	9.00	25.00	1,100.00
1845	1564	4.50	8.00	400.00
1846	27	60.00	100.00	1,500.00
1847	1274	4.50	8.00	400.00
1848	668	4.50	8.00	400.00
1848O	600	7.50	18.00	600.00
1849 over 48, All Kinds	1309	6.00	10.00	400.00
1849 over 46	—	6.50	11.50	400.00
1849	—	4.50	8.00	400.00
1849O	140	30.00	70.00	2,000.00
1850	955	4.50	8.00	400.00

	Mintage in Thousands	Good	Fine	Unc.
1850O	690	6.00	12.00	600.00
1851	781	4.50	8.00	400.00
1851O	860	6.00	11.00	500.00
1852	1001	4.50	8.00	400.00
1852O	260	7.00	20.00	1,100.00
1853 No Arrows	135	12.00	25.00	1,000.00
1853O No Arrows	160	75.00	200.00	3,000.00

	Mintage in Thousands	Good	Fine	Unc.	Proof
1853 With Arrows	13210	5.00	10.00	750.00	—
1853O	2200	5.00	10.00	900.00	—
1854	5740	5.00	10.00	700.00	—
1854O	1560	5.00	10.00	800.00	
1855	1750	5.00	10.00	750.00	1,800.00
1855O	600	7.00	14.00	850.00	—
1856 No Arrows	4880	5.00	10.00	400.00	1,300.00
1856O	1100	5.00	10.00	400.00	—
1857	7280	5.00	10.00	400.00	1,300.00
1857O	1380	5.00	10.00	400.00	—
1858	3500	5.00	10.00	400.00	1,250.00
1858O	1660	5.00	10.00	400.00	—
1859	340	5.00	10.00	400.00	1,250.00
1859O	560	5.00	10.00	400.00	—
1860	799	5.00	10.00	400.00	750.00
1860O	1060	5.00	10.00	400.00	—
1861	3361	5.00	10.00	400.00	750.00
1862	1493	5.00	10.00	400.00	750.00
1863	18	22.00	35.00	380.00	900.00
1863S	100	17.00	25.00	415.00	—
1864	48	60.00	100.00	600.00	1,100.00
1864S	90	15.00	30.00	460.00	—
1865	14	20.00	30.00	350.00	800.00
1865S	120	10.00	20.00	350.00	—
1866	11	25.00	35.00	350.00	800.00
1866S	120	10.00	20.00	350.00	
1867	9	30.00	40.00	400.00	900.00
1867S	120	10.00	20.00	325.00	—
1868	89	7.00	15.00	300.00	750.00
1868S	280	5.00	10.00	500.00	—
1869	209	5.00	10.00	300.00	750.00
1869S	230	5.00	10.00	300.00	—
1870	537	5.00	10.00	300.00	750.00
1871	1874	4.00	6.00	300.00	700.00
1871S	161	10.00	20.00	300.00	—
1872	2948	4.00	6.00	300.00	700.00
1872S Mint Mark within Wreath	837	4.50	8.00	300.00	—
1872 Mint Mark Below	—	4.50	8.00	300.00	—
1873	713	4.00	6.00	300.00	750.00
1873S	324	4.50	8.00	300.00	—

31.
DIMES—
1796–Date

DRAPED BUST TYPE

1796–1797   **1798–1807**

	Mintage in Thousands	Good	Fine	Unc.
1796	22	1,500.00	2,300.00	9,000.00
1797 16 Stars, All Kinds	25	1,300.00	2,100.00	8,500.00
1797 13 Stars	—	1,300.00	2,100.00	8,500.00
1798 over 97, 13 Stars on Reverse, All Kinds	28	—	1,000.00	—
1798 over 97, 16 Stars on Reverse	—	550.00	1,100.00	5,000.00
1798	—	550.00	1,100.00	5,000.00
1800	22	550.00	1,100.00	5,000.00
1801	35	550.00	1,100.00	5,000.00
1802	11	550.00	1,100.00	5,000.00
1803	33	550.00	1,100.00	5,000.00
1804 13 Stars on Reverse, All Kinds	8	550.00	1,100.00	5,000.00
1804 14 Stars on Reverse	—	550.00	1,100.00	5,000.00
1805	121	550.00	1,100.00	5,000.00
1807	165	550.00	1,100.00	5,000.00

LIBERTY CAP TYPE

	Mintage in Thousands	Good	Fine	Unc.
1809	51	60.00	150.00	2,250.00
1811 over 9	65	50.00	90.00	2,000.00

	Mintage in Thousands	Good	Fine	Unc.
1814	422	22.00	40.00	1,700.00
1820	943	20.00	40.00	1,700.00
1821	1187	20.00	40.00	1,700.00
1822	100	50.00	150.00	2,200.00
1823 over 22, All Kinds	440	20.00	40.00	1,900.00
1824 over 22	—	30.00	60.00	2,300.00
1825	510	20.00	40.00	1,700.00
1827	1215	20.00	40.00	1,700.00
1828	125	22.00	40.00	1,700.00
1829	770	15.00	22.00	1,200.00
1830	510	15.00	22.00	1,200.00
1831	771	15.00	22.00	1,200.00
1832	523	15.00	22.00	1,200.00
1833	485	15.00	22.00	1,200.00
1834	635	15.00	22.00	1,200.00
1835	1410	15.00	22.00	1,000.00
1836	1190	15.00	22.00	1,200.00
1837	1042	15.00	22.00	1,200.00

LIBERTY SEATED TYPE

No Stars   Stars

	Good	Fine	Unc.
1837 No Stars	(included above) 35.00	75.00	1,750.00
1838O No Stars	406 50.00	135.00	2,750.00
1838 With Stars, All Kinds	1993 5.00	9.50	600.00
1838 With Partial Drapery	— 10.00	35.00	500.00
1839	1053 5.00	8.50	600.00
1839O	1323 5.00	10.00	500.00
1840	1359 5.00	8.00	500.00
1840O	1175 6.00	13.00	500.00
1841	1623 4.00	7.00	500.00
1841O	2008 4.00	7.00	500.00
			500.00

	Mintage in Thousands	Good	Fine	Unc.
1842	1888	4.00	7.00	200.00
1842O	2020	5.00	9.00	250.00
1843	1370	4.00	7.00	200.00
1843O	150	25.00	100.00	3,000.00
1844	73	23.00	60.00	850.00
1845	1755	4.00	7.00	200.00
1845O	230	20.00	25.00	1,500.00
1846	31	30.00	60.00	600.00
1847	245	6.00	13.00	250.00
1848	452	5.00	10.00	250.00
1849	839	4.00	7.00	250.00
1849O	300	10.00	20.00	500.00
1850	1932	4.00	7.00	200.00
1850O	510	7.00	15.00	300.00
1851	1027	4.00	7.00	200.00
1851O	400	7.00	12.00	325.00

The Unc. column values printed along the right edge: 500.00, 500.00, 500.00, 500.00, 3,000.00, 850.00, 500.00, 1,500.00, 600.00, 500.00, 500.00, 500.00, 500.00, 500.00, 500.00, 500.00, 500.00

110

	Mintage in Thousands	Good	Fine	Unc	Proof
1852	1536	4.00	7.00	500.00	—
1852O	430	8.00	18.00	600.00	—
1853 (No Arrows)	95	30.00	50.00	800.00	—
1853 With Arrows	12,078	4.00	9.00	750.00	—
1853O	1100	6.00	12.00	750.00	—
1854	4470	4.00	9.00	750.00	—
1854O	1770	5.00	12.00	750.00	—
1855	2075	4.00	9.00	750.00	1,900.00
1856 No Arrows	5780	4.00	7.00	500.00	1,650.00
1856O	1180	4.00	7.00	500.00	—
1856S	70	30.00	80.00	1,500.00	—
1857	5580	4.00	7.00	500.00	1,250.00
1857O	1540	4.00	8.00	500.00	—
1858	1540	4.00	7.00	500.00	1,250.00
1858O	290	6.00	10.00	500.00	—
1858S	60	25.00	60.00	900.00	—
1859	430	4.00	7.00	500.00	1,250.00
1859O	480	4.00	8.00	500.00	—
1859S	60	25.00	55.00	800.00	—
1860S	140	10.00	30.00	650.00	—

1860–1891

	Mintage in Thousands	Good	Fine	Unc	Proof
1860	607	4.00	7.00	350.00	750.00
1860O	40	300.00	750.00	—	—
1861	1884	4.00	7.00	350.00	750.00
1861S	173	15.00	40.00	600.00	—
1862	848	4.00	7.00	350.00	750.00
1862S	181	10.00	30.00	375.00	—
1863	14	30.00	50.00	600.00	750.00
1863S	158	12.50	35.00	500.00	—
1864	11	35.00	60.00	550.00	1,100.00
1864S	230	10.00	25.00	600.00	—
1865	11	30.00	60.00	500.00	1,000.00
1865S	175	10.00	30.00	500.00	—
1866	9	40.00	80.00	500.00	1,000.00
1866S	135	10.00	30.00	450.00	—
1867	7	40.00	80.00	500.00	1,000.00
1867S	140	10.00	30.00	400.00	—
1868	465	4.00	7.00	350.00	750.00
1868S	260	8.00	20.00	350.00	—
1869	257	4.00	7.00	350.00	750.00
1869S	450	7.00	14.00	350.00	—
1870	472	4.00	7.00	350.00	750.00
1870S	50	55.00	100.00	600.00	—
1871	908	4.00	7.00	350.00	750.00
1871CC	20	125.00	350.00	2,600.00	—
1871S	320	9.00	25.00	450.00	—
1872	2396	4.00	7.00	350.00	750.00

	Mintage in Thousands	Good	Fine	Unc.	Proof
1872CC	24	85.00	190.00	2,000.00	—
1872S	190	12.50	25.00	350.00	—
1873	1569	4.00	7.00	350.00	700.00
1873CC No Arrows (Unique)	12	—	—	—	—
1873 Arrows at date	2379	10.00	22.00	400.00	1,350.00
1873CC	19	350.00	700.00	3,250.00	—
1873S	455	15.00	35.00	450.00	—
1874	2941	10.00	22.00	450.00	1,350.00
1874CC	11	110.00	225.00	2,900.00	—
1874S	240	15.00	35.00	450.00	—
1875 Arrows at Date Removed	10,351	4.00	7.00	350.00	700.00
1875CC Under Wreath, All Kinds	4645	4.00	7.00	350.00	—
1875CC In Wreath	—	4.00	7.00	350.00	—
1875S Under Wreath, All Kinds	9070	4.00	7.00	350.00	—
1875S In Wreath	—	4.00	7.00	350.00	—
1876	11461	4.00	7.00	350.00	700.00
1876CC	8270	4.00	7.00	350.00	—
1876S	10,420	4.00	7.00	350.00	—
1877	7311	4.00	7.00	350.00	700.00
1877CC	7700	4.00	7.00	350.00	—
1877S	2340	4.00	7.00	350.00	—
1878	1679	4.00	7.00	350.00	700.00
1878CC	200	15.00	30.00	350.00	—
1879	15	25.00	50.00	350.00	700.00
1880	37	22.50	45.00	350.00	700.00
1881	25	23.00	45.00	350.00	700.00
1882	3911	4.00	7.00	350.00	700.00
1883	7676	4.00	7.00	350.00	700.00
1884	3366	4.00	7.00	350.00	700.00
1884S	565	8.00	15.00	350.00	—
1885	2533	4.00	7.00	350.00	700.00
1885S	44	75.00	150.00	1,000.00	—
1886	6378	4.00	7.00	350.00	700.00
1886S	207	7.00	15.00	350.00	—
1887	11,284	4.00	7.00	350.00	700.00
1887S	4454	4.00	7.00	350.00	—
1888	5496	4.00	7.00	350.00	700.00
1888S	1720	4.00	7.00	350.00	—
1889	7381	4.00	7.00	350.00	700.00
1889S	973	7.50	15.00	350.00	—
1890	9912	4.00	7.00	350.00	700.00
1890S	1423	4.00	7.00	350.00	—
1891	15,311	4.00	7.00	350.00	700.00
1891O	4540	4.00	7.00	350.00	—
1891S	3196	4.00	7.00	350.00	—

BARBER OR LIBERTY HEAD TYPE

	Mintage in Thousands	Good	Fine	Unc.	Proof
1892	12,121	1.50	4.50	250.00	700.00
1892O	3842	2.75	7.00	300.00	—
1892S	991	17.00	27.00	325.00	—
1893	3341	2.75	7.00	300.00	700.00
1893O	1760	8.00	16.00	400.00	—
1893S	2491	4.00	9.00	325.00	—
1894	1331	5.00	11.00	325.00	700.00
1894O	720	20.00	70.00	1,750.00	—
1894S (Very rare)	24 Pieces	—	—	—	—
1895	691	40.00	60.00	700.00	950.00
1895O	440	110.00	150.00	2,000.00	—
1895S	1120	10.00	20.00	350.00	—
1896	2001	3.50	9.00	280.00	700.00
1896O	610	30.00	60.00	900.00	—
1896S	575	25.00	60.00	700.00	—
1897	10,869	1.50	3.00	250.00	700.00
1897O	666	21.00	45.00	1,300.00	—
1897S	1343	6.00	15.00	350.00	—
1898	16,321	1.50	3.00	250.00	700.00
1898O	2130	3.00	10.00	450.00	—
1898S	1703	3.00	9.00	300.00	—
1899	19,581	1.50	3.00	250.00	700.00
1899O	2650	3.00	9.00	425.00	—
1899S	1867	3.50	9.00	300.00	—
1900	17,601	1.50	3.00	250.00	700.00
1900O	2010	4.00	12.00	450.00	—
1900S	5168	1.50	5.00	300.00	—
1901	18,860	1.50	3.00	250.00	700.00
1901O	5620	1.50	6.00	450.00	—
1901S	593	25.00	80.00	1,300.00	—
1902	21,381	1.50	3.00	250.00	700.00
1902O	4500	1.50	6.00	350.00	—
1902S	2070	3.00	8.00	400.00	—
1903	19,501	1.50	3.00	250.00	700.00
1903O	8180	1.50	4.00	350.00	—
1903S	613	16.00	35.00	1,175.00	—
1904	14,601	1.50	3.00	250.00	700.00
1904S	800	12.00	21.00	1,150.00	—
1905	14,552	1.50	3.00	250.00	700.00
1905O	3400	1.50	6.50	325.00	—
1905S	6855	1.50	3.00	300.00	—
1906	19,958	1.50	3.00	250.00	700.00
1906D	4060	1.50	4.00	280.00	—
1906O	2610	2.00	7.00	300.00	—
1906S	3137	1.50	3.25	325.00	—
1907	22,221	150	3.00	240.00	700.00
1907D	4080	1.50	4.00	280.00	—
1907O	5058	1.50	4.50	270.00	—
1907S	3178	4.00	3.75	375.00	—

	Mintage in Thousands	Good	Fine	Unc.	Proof
1908	10,601	1.50	3.00	250.00	700.00
1908D	7490	1.50	3.00	250.00	—
1908O	1789	2.75	8.00	360.00	—
1908S	3220	1.50	4.00	350.00	—
1909	10,241	1.50	3.00	250.00	700.00
1909D	954	2.50	11.00	375.00	—
1909O	2287	1.75	7.00	300.00	—
1909S	1000	3.00	11.00	375.00	—
1910	11,521	1.50	3.00	250.00	700.00
1910D	3490	1.50	3.00	350.00	—
1910S	1240	2.00	5.50	325.00	—
1911	18,871	1.50	3.00	250.00	700.00
1911D	17,209	1.50	3.00	250.00	—
1911S	3520	1.50	3.00	290.00	—
1912	19,351	1.50	3.00	250.00	700.00
1912D	11,760	1.50	3.00	250.00	—
1912S	3420	1.50	4.00	285.00	—
1913	19,761	1.50	3.00	250.00	800.00
1913S	510	7.00	25.00	550.00	—
1914	17,361	1.50	3.00	250.00	900.00
1914D	11,908	1.50	3.00	250.00	—
1914S	2100	1.50	3.50	300.00	—
1915	5620	1.50	3.00	250.00	400.00
1915S	960	1.75	5.50	325.00	—
1916	18,490	1.50	3.00	250.00	—
1916S	5820	1.50	3.00	250.00	—

MERCURY TYPE

	Mintage in Thousands	Good	Fine	Ex. Fine	Unc.
1916	22,180	2.50	2.00	5.00	28.00
1916D	264	350.00	750.00	1,500.00	2,300.00
1916S	10,450	1.75	5.00	10.00	45.00
1917	55,230	1.50	2.00	4.00	25.00
1917D	9402	2.00	7.00	25.00	135.00
1917S	27,330	1.50	2.00	8.00	40.00
1918	26,680	1.50	3.00	22.50	70.00
1918D	22,675	1.50	3.50	20.00	90.00
1918S	19,300	1.50	2.00	15.00	75.00
1919	35,740	1.50	2.00	7.50	40.00
1919D	9939	1.50	6.00	45.00	175.00
1919S	8850	1.50	6.00	50.00	190.00
1920	59,030	1.50	2.00	4.00	25.00
1920D	19,171	1.50	2.00	10.00	85.00
1920S	13,820	1.50	2.00	9.00	85.00
1921	1230	18.00	45.00	300.00	1,300.00
1921D	1080	27.00	70.00	300.00	1,150.00
1923	50,130	1.50	2.00	3.00	22.50

	Mintage in Thousands	Good	Fine	Ex. Fine	Unc.
1923S	6440	1.50	3.50	20.00	125.00
1924	24,010	1.50	2.00	4.00	42.50
1924D	6810	1.50	3.00	15.00	125.00
1924S	7120	1.50	2.25	17.00	125.00
1925	25,610	1.50	2.00	4.00	45.00
1925D	5117	2.00	8.50	60.00	275.00
1925S	5850	1.50	2.00	20.00	150.00
1926	32,160	1.50	2.00	3.00	24.00
1926D	6828	1.50	2.00	12.00	80.00
1926S	1520	5.00	10.00	55.00	50.00
1927	28,080	1.50	2.00	3.00	20.00
1927D	4812	1.50	5.00	30.00	250.00
1927S	4770	1.50	2.00	15.00	110.00
1928	19,480	1.50	2.00	3.00	22.00
1928D	4161	1.50	3.75	25.00	175.00
1928S	7400	1.50	2.00	9.00	75.00
1929	25,970	1.50	2.00	3.00	18.00
1929D	5034	1.50	2.00	4.75	25.00
1929S	4730	1.50	2.00	3.75	45.00
1930	6770	1.50	2.00	4.00	25.00
1930S	1843	2.00	3.00	9.50	110.00
1931	3150	1.50	2.00	5.00	40.00
1931D	1260	5.00	7.50	15.00	110.00
1931S	1800	2.00	3.00	10.00	100.00
1934	24,080	1.50	2.00	3.00	20.00
1934D	6772	1.50	2.00	3.00	55.00
1935	58,830	1.50	2.00	3.00	11.00
1935D	10,477	1.50	2.00	3.50	110.00
1935S	15,840	1.50	2.00	3.00	35.00

	Mintage in Thousands	Good	Fine	Ex. Fine	Unc.	Proof
1936	87,504	1.50	2.00	3.00	11.00	1,000.00
1936D	16,132	1.50	2.00	3.50	50.00	—
1936S	9210	1.50	2.00	3.50	25.00	—
1937	56,866	1.50	2.00	3.00	9.00	750.00
1937D	14,146	1.50	2.00	3.00	40.00	—
1937S	9740	1.50	2.00	3.00	32.00	—
1938	22,199	1.50	2.00	3.00	12.00	500.00
1938D	5537	1.50	2.00	3.00	40.00	—
1938S	8090	1.50	2.00	3.00	17.00	—
1939	67,749	1.50	2.00	3.00	8.00	300.00
1939D	24,394	1.50	2.00	3.00	8.50	—
1939S	10,540	1.50	2.00	3.00	28.00	—
1940	65,362	1.50	2.00	3.00	6.00	175.00
1940D	21,198	1.50	2.00	3.00	18.00	—
1940S	21,560	1.50	2.00	3.00	8.00	—
1941	175,107	1.50	2.00	3.00	5.00	125.00
1941D	45,634	1.50	2.00	3.00	20.00	—
1941S	43,090	1.50	2.00	3.00	9.00	—
1942 over 41, All Kinds	205,432	225.00	275.00	325.00	—	—
1942	—	1.50	2.00	3.00	5.00	125.00
1942D, 2 over 1	—	250.00	300.00	350.00	—	—
1942D	60,740	1.50	2.00	3.00	13.00	—
1942S	49,300	1.50	2.00	3.00	25.00	—

	Mintage in Thousands	Good	Fine	Ex. Fine	Unc.
1943	191,710	1.50	2.00	3.00	5.00
1943D	71,949	1.50	2.00	3.00	7.00
1943S	60,400	1.50	2.00	3.00	15.00
1944	231,410	1.50	2.00	3.00	5.00
1944D	62,224	1.50	2.00	3.00	8.00
1944S	49,490	1.50	2.00	3.00	12.00
1945	159,130	1.50	2.00	3.00	5.00
1945D	40,245	1.50	2.00	3.00	10.00
1945S	41,920	1.50	2.00	3.00	8.00

ROOSEVELT TYPE

	Mintage in Thousands	V. Good	Fine	Ex. Fine	Unc.
1946	255,250	1.50	1.75	2.00	2.50
1946D	61,044	1.50	1.75	2.00	3.50
1946S	27,900	1.50	1.75	2.00	4.50
1947	121,520	1.50	1.75	2.00	4.00
1947D	46,835	1.50	1.75	2.00	12.00
1947S	34,840	1.50	1.75	2.00	4.00
1948	74,950	1.50	1.75	2.00	5.00
1948D	52,841	1.50	1.75	2.00	15.00
1948S	35,520	1.50	1.75	2.00	7.00
1949	30,940	1.50	1.75	2.00	25.00
1949D	26,034	1.50	1.75	2.00	10.00
1949S	13,510	1.50	1.75	2.00	40.00
1950	50,182	1.50	1.75	2.00	5.00
1950D	46,803	1.50	1.75	2.00	5.00
1950S	20,440	1.50	1.75	2.00	20.00
1951	103,938	1.50	1.75	2.00	3.00
1951D	56,529	1.50	1.75	2.00	3.00
1951S	31,630	1.50	1.75	2.00	15.00
1952	99,122	1.50	1.75	2.00	3.00
1952D	122,100	1.50	1.75	2.00	4.00
1952S	44,420	1.50	1.75	2.00	6.00
1953	53,619	1.50	1.75	2.00	4.00
1953D	136,433	1.50	1.75	2.00	4.00
1953S	39,180	1.50	1.75	2.00	3.00
1954	114,244	1.50	1.75	2.00	2.50
1954D	106,397	1.50	1.75	2.00	2.50
1954S	22,860	1.50	1.75	2.00	2.50
1955	12,828	1.50	1.75	2.00	4.00
1955D	13,959	1.50	1.75	2.00	3.50
1955S	18,510	1.50	1.75	2.00	3.50
1956	109,309	1.50	1.75	2.00	2.50
1956D	108,015	1.50	1.75	2.00	3.00
1957	167,408	1.50	1.75	2.00	2.50
1957D	133,354	1.50	1.75	2.00	3.50
1958	32,786	1.50	1.75	2.00	2.50
1958D	136,565	1.50	1.75	2.00	2.50

	Mintage in Thousands	V. Good	Fine	Ex. Fine	Unc.
1959	86,929	1.50	1.75	2.00	2.25
1959D	164,920	1.50	1.75	2.00	2.25
1960	72,082	1.50	1.75	2.00	2.25
1960D	200,160	1.50	1.75	2.00	2.25
1961	96,758	1.50	1.75	2.00	2.25
1961D	209,147	1.50	1.75	2.00	2.25
1962	75,668	1.50	1.75	2.00	2.25
1962D	334,948	1.50	1.75	2.00	2.25
1963	126,726	1.50	1.75	2.00	2.25
1963D	421,477	1.50	1.75	2.00	2.25
1964	933,311	1.50	1.75	2.00	2.25
1964D	1,357,517	1.50	1.75	2.00	2.25
1965	1,652,141	—	—	—	.25
1966	1,382,735	—	—	—	.25
1967	2,244,007	—	—	—	.25
1968	424,470	—	—	—	.25
1968D	480,748	—	—	—	.25
1968S Proof only	3042	—	—	—	1.25
1969	145,790	—	—	—	.25
1969D	563,324	—	—	—	.25
1969S Proof only	2935	—	—	—	1.00

	Mintage in Thousands	Fine	Ex. Fine	Unc.
1970	345,570	—	—	.25
1970D	754,942	—	—	.25
1970S Proof only	2,633	—	—	1.00
1971	162,690	—	—	.25
1971D	377,914	—	—	.25
1971S Proof only	3,224	—	—	1.00
1972	431,540	—	—	.25
1972D	330,290	—	—	.25
1972S Proof only	3,268	—	—	1.00
1973	315,670	—	—	.25
1973D	455,032	—	—	.25
1973S Proof only	2,770	—	—	1.25
1974	470,248	—	—	.25
1974D	571,083	—	—	.25
1974S Proof only	2,617	—	—	1.50
1975	585,678	—	—	.25
1975D	313,705	—	—	.25
1975S Proof only	2,909	—	—	1.50
1976 P-D	1,263,983	—	—	.25
1976S Proof only	4,150	—	—	1.00
1977 P-D	1,173,537	—	—	.25
1977S Proof only	3,251	—	—	.75
1978 P-D	946,828	—	—	.25
1978S Proof only	3,128	—	—	1.00
1979 P&D	706,361	—	—	.25
1979S Proof only	3,677	—	—	1.25
1980 P&D	—	—	—	.25
1980S Proof only	—	—	—	1.00
1981 P&D	—	—	—	.25
1981S Proof only	—	—	—	1.50

32.

TWENTY-CENT PIECES—
1875–1878

	Mintage in Thousands	Good	Fine	V. Fine	Unc.	Proof
1875.................	40	45.00	70.00	90.00	1,100.00	1,700.00
1875CC	133	40.00	70.00	85.00	1,100.00	—
1875S...............	1155	35.00	55.00	80.00	1,100.00	—
1876.................	16	60.00	80.00	140.00	1,200.00	1,750.00
1876CC (14 known).........	10	—	—	—	—	—
1877.................	1	—	—	—	—	2,100.00
1878..................	1	—	—	—	—	2,000.00

33.

QUARTER-DOLLARS—
1796–Date

DRAPED BUST TYPE

1796   1804–1807

	Mintage in Thousands	Good	Fine	Unc.
1796...	6	2,700.00	4,500.00	25,000.00
1804...	7	200.00	500.00	—

	Mintage in Thousands	Good	Fine	Unc.
1805...	121	150.00	425.00	6,000.00
1806 over 5, All Kinds	206	150.00	425.00	7,000.00
1806...	—	150.00	400.00	6,500.00
1807...	221	150.00	400.00	6,000.00

LIBERTY HEAD TYPE

1815–1828   1831–1838

1815...	89	38.00	75.00	3,500.00
1818 over 15, All Kinds	361	38.00	75.00	3,350.00
1818...	—	30.00	65.00	3,200.00
1819...	144	30.00	65.00	2,600.00
1820...	127	30.00	65.00	2,600.00
1821...	217	30.00	65.00	2,600.00
1822, All Kinds	64	30.00	75.00	2,800.00
1822 25 over 50c	—	200.00	375.00	4,000.00
1823 over 22, All Kinds	18	1,000.00	2,000.00	—
1824 over 2	—	40.00	100.00	3,000.00
1825 over 22, All Kinds	168	30.00	65.00	3,950.00
1825 over 23	—	30.00	65.00	2,800.00
1825 over 24	—	30.00	65.00	3,000.00
1827 Original, curled base 2 in 25c, All Kinds	4	—	—	45,000.00
1827 Restrike; square base 2 in 25c	—	—	—	19,000.00
1828, All Kinds	102	30.00	65.00	2,750.00
1828 25 over 50c	—	75.00	150.00	3,250.00
1831...	398	25.00	45.00	1,500.00
1832...	320	25.00	45.00	1,500.00
1833...	156	25.00	45.00	1,500.00
1834...	286	25.00	45.00	1,500.00
1835...	1952	25.00	45.00	1,500.00
1836...	472	25.00	45.00	1,500.00
1837...	252	25.00	45.00	1,500.00
1838...	832	25.00	45.00	1,500.00

LIBERTY SEATED TYPE

1838–1865

1866–1891

	Mintage in Thousands	Good	Fine	Unc.
1838 No Drapery	(included above)	9.00	22.00	2,500.00
1839 No Drapery	491	8.00	17.00	2,500.00
1840O No Drapery	425	8.00	17.00	2,500.00
1840 Drapery	188	7.00	15.00	1,100.00
1840O Drapery	(included above)	7.00	15.00	800.00
1841	120	15.00	30.00	675.00
1841O	452	7.00	14.00	675.00
1842	88	25.00	60.00	800.00
1842O	769	8.00	16.00	675.00
1843	646	7.00	12.00	675.00
1843O	968	7.00	12.00	675.00
1844	421	7.00	11.00	675.00
1844O	740	7.00	11.00	675.00
1845	922	7.00	11.00	675.00
1846	510	7.00	11.00	675.00
1847	734	7.00	11.00	675.00
1847O	368	8.00	12.00	675.00
1848	146	7.00	18.00	675.00
1849	340	7.00	11.00	675.00
1849O	—	100.00	300.00	2,500.00
1850	191	7.00	15.00	675.00
1850O	412	12.00	25.00	675.00
1851	160	9.00	20.00	675.00
1851O	88	40.00	95.00	950.00
1852	177	14.00	30.00	675.00
1852O	96	100.00	250.00	1,300.00
1853 over 52. No Arrows or Rays	44	80.00	175.00	1,250.00

	Mintage in Thousands	Good	Fine	Unc.	Proof
1853 Arrows and Rays	15,210	7.00	18.00	1,500.00	—
1853O	1332	10.00	25.00	1,800.00	—
1854 Arrows, no Rays	12,380	7.00	12.00	1,000.00	—
1854O	1484	7.00	15.00	1,000.00	—
1855	2857	7.00	13.00	1,000.00	—
1855O	176	40.00	85.00	2,500.00	—
1855S	396	35.00	75.00	2,300.00	—
1856 No Arrows	7264	7.00	11.00	600.00	1,850.00
1856O	968	7.00	12.00	600.00	—
1856S	286	20.00	40.00	900.00	—
1857	9644	7.00	11.00	600.00	1,750.00

	Mintage in Thousands	Good	Fine	Unc.	Proof
1857O	1180	7.00	12.00	650.00	—
1857S	82	23.00	50.00	1,850.00	—
1858	7368	7.00	11.00	650.00	900.00
1858O	520	7.00	12.00	650.00	—
1858S	121	30.00	45.00	800.00	—
1859	1344	7.00	11.00	650.00	800.00
1859O	260	7.00	12.00	650.00	—
1859S	80	35.00	90.00	1,100.00	—
1860	805	7.00	11.00	650.00	700.00
1860O	388	7.00	12.00	650.00	—
1860S	56	40.00	100.00	900.00	—
1861	4855	7.00	11.00	650.00	700.00
1861S	96	20.00	40.00	1,400.00	—
1862	933	7.00	11.00	650.00	700.00
1862S	67	18.00	30.00	1,250.00	—
1863	192	10.00	30.00	650.00	700.00
1864	94	20.00	45.00	750.00	800.00
1864S	20	90.00	200.00	2,350.00	—
1865	59	25.00	55.00	650.00	700.00
1865S	41	25.00	55.00	1,700.00	—
1866	18	45.00	90.00	650.00	700.00
1866S	28	30.00	70.00	1,400.00	—
1867	21	35.00	90.00	650.00	700.00
1867S	48	30.00	60.00	1,400.00	—
1868	30	35.00	75.00	650.00	700.00
1868S	96	20.00	50.00	1,000.00	—
1869	17	40.00	90.00	700.00	700.00
1869S	76	20.00	50.00	1,100.00	—
1870	87	20.00	45.00	650.00	700.00
1870CC	8	325.00	750.00	3,000.00	—
1871	119	7.00	15.00	650.00	700.00
1871CC	11	200.00	500.00	2,500.00	—
1871S	31	60.00	150.00	1,100.00	—
1872	183	7.00	11.00	650.00	700.00
1872CC	9	175.00	275.00	3,500.00	—
1872S	83	70.00	190.00	1,150.00	—
1873 No Arrows	213	10.00	25.00	650.00	700.00
1873 Arrows	1272	17.00	25.00	650.00	800.00
1873CC	12	350.00	750.00	3,500.00	—
1873S	156	20.00	40.00	700.00	—
1874	472	17.00	25.00	650.00	800.00
1874S	392	20.00	40.00	650.00	—
1875 Arrows Removed	4294	7.00	10.00	650.00	700.00
1875CC	140	22.00	55.00	900.00	—
1875S	680	10.00	25.00	650.00	—
1876	17.817	7.00	10.00	650.00	700.00
1876CC	4944	7.00	10.00	650.00	—
1876S	8596	7.00	10.00	650.00	—
1877	10.912	7.00	10.00	650.00	700.00
1877CC	4192	7.00	10.00	650.00	—
1877S	8996	7.00	10.00	650.00	—
1878	2261	7.00	10.00	650.00	700.00
1878CC	996	8.00	15.00	650.00	—
1878S	140	100.00	250.00	1,100.00	—
1879	15	40.00	60.00	650.00	700.00
1880	15	40.00	60.00	650.00	700.00
1881	13	40.00	60.00	650.00	700.00
1882	16	40.00	60.00	650.00	700.00

	Mintage in Thousands	Good	Fine	Unc.	Proof
1883	15	40.00	60.00	650.00	700.00
1884	9	50.00	80.00	700.00	700.00
1885	15	40.00	60.00	650.00	700.00
1886	6	55.00	90.00	850.00	875.00
1887	11	45.00	85.00	650.00	700.00
1888	11	45.00	80.00	650.00	700.00
1888S	1216	7.00	15.00	650.00	—
1889	13	40.00	60.00	650.00	700.00
1890	81	20.00	40.00	650.00	700.00
1891	3921	7.00	10.00	650.00	700.00
1891O	68	80.00	150.00	2,250.00	—
1891S	2216	7.00	10.00	650.00	—

BARBER OR LIBERTY HEAD TYPE

	Mintage in Thousands	Good	Fine	Ex. Fine	Unc.	Proof
1892	8237	4.00	8.00	30.00	350.00	800.00
1892O	2640	4.00	9.00	35.00	400.00	—
1892S	964	10.00	25.00	65.00	600.00	—
1893	5445	4.00	8.00	35.00	350.00	800.00
1893O	3396	4.00	9.50	35.00	450.00	—
1893S	1455	5.00	11.50	35.00	460.00	—
1894	3433	4.00	8.00	33.00	400.00	800.00
1894O	2852	4.00	8.00	35.00	510.00	—
1894S	2649	4.00	9.50	35.00	500.00	—
1895	4441	4.00	8.00	30.00	390.00	800.00
1895O	2816	4.00	8.00	35.00	525.00	—
1895S	1765	4.00	10.00	40.00	440.00	—
1896	3875	4.00	8.00	35.00	400.00	800.00
1896O	1484	4.00	17.00	55.00	1,700.00	—
1896S	188	180.00	425.00	1,100.00	4,000.00	—
1897	8141	4.00	8.00	30.00	350.00	800.00
1897O	1415	6.00	17.00	50.00	1,750.00	—
1897S	542	10.00	20.00	65.00	650.00	—
1898	11,101	4.00	8.00	30.00	350.00	800.00
1898O	1868	4.00	10.00	35.00	700.00	—
1898S	1021	4.50	11.00	35.00	550.00	—
1899	12,625	4.00	8.00	30.00	350.00	800.00
1899O	2644	4.00	8.00	35.00	575.00	—
1899S	708	7.00	15.00	40.00	550.00	—
1900	10,017	4.00	8.00	30.00	350.00	800.00
1900O	3416	4.00	11.00	35.00	750.00	—
1900S	1859	4.00	8.00	35.00	500.00	—
1901	8893	4.00	8.00	30.00	350.00	800.00
1901O	1612	7.50	25.00	95.00	1,500.00	—
1901S	73	850.00	1,350.00	2,500.00	15,000.00	—

	Mintage in Thousands	Good	Fine	Ex. Fine	Unc.	Proof
1902	12.198	3.50	7.50	30.00	350.00	800.00
1902O	4748	3.50	9.00	35.00	600.00	—
1902S	1525	5.00	12.50	45.00	500.00	—
1903	9670	3.50	7.50	30.00	350.00	800.00
1903O	3500	3.50	8.50	40.00	450.00	—
1903S	1036	4.00	17.50	55.00	510.00	—
1904	9589	3.50	7.50	35.00	350.00	800.00
1904O	2456	3.50	15.00	55.00	1,250.00	—
1905	4968	3.50	7.50	30.00	350.00	800.00
1905O	1230	4.50	15.00	35.00	400.00	—
1905S	1884	3.50	8.50	35.00	350.00	—
1906	3656	3.50	7.50	30.00	350.00	800.00
1906D	3280	3.50	7.50	30.00	350.00	—
1906O	2056	3.50	7.50	30.00	400.00	—
1907	7193	3.50	7.50	30.00	350.00	800.00
1907D	2484	3.50	7.50	30.00	400.00	—
1907O	4560	3.50	7.50	30.00	375.00	—
1907S	1360	3.50	7.50	30.00	500.00	—
1908	4233	3.50	7.50	30.00	350.00	800.00
1908D	5788	3.50	7.50	30.00	350.00	—
1908O	6244	3.50	7.50	30.00	400.00	—
1908S	784	6.00	10.00	38.00	600.00	—
1909	9269	3.50	7.50	30.00	350.00	800.00
1909D	5114	3.50	7.50	30.00	350.00	—
1909O	712	10.00	32.50	90.00	1,000.00	—
1909S	1348	3.50	7.50	30.00	400.00	—
1910	2245	3.50	7.50	30.00	350.00	800.00
1910D	1500	3.50	7.50	30.00	450.00	—
1911	3721	3.50	7.50	30.00	350.00	800.00
1911D	934	3.50	7.50	30.00	350.00	—
1911S	988	3.50	7.50	30.00	425.00	—
1912	4401	3.50	7.50	30.00	350.00	800.00
1912S	708	3.50	8.00	30.00	450.00	—
1913	485	7.00	25.00	210.00	2,250.00	2,400.00
1913D	1451	3.50	7.50	35.00	350.00	—
1913S	40	250.00	450.00	1,100.00	4,500.00	—
1914	6245	3.50	7.50	30.00	350.00	900.00
1914D	3046	3.50	7.50	30.00	375.00	—
1914S	264	10.00	20.00	90.00	1,200.00	—
1915	3480	3.50	7.50	30.00	350.00	1,100.00
1915D	3694	3.50	7.50	30.00	350.00	—
1915S	708	3.50	7.50	35.00	380.00	—
1916	1788	3.50	7.50	30.00	350.00	—
1916D	6541	3.50	7.50	30.00	350.00	—

STANDING LIBERTY TYPE

1916–1917

1917–1930

123

	Mintage in Thousands	Good	Fine	Ex. Fine	Unc.
1916	52	800.00	1,500.00	2,250.00	3,500.00
1917 Type 1	8792	7.00	10.00	38.00	225.00
1917D	1509	10.00	15.00	85.00	250.00
1917S	1952	10.00	12.00	75.00	250.00
1917 Type 2	13,880	8.00	10.00	25.00	120.00
1917D	6224	12.00	25.00	70.00	160.00
1917S	5552	11.00	20.00	50.00	160.00
1918	14,240	10.00	13.00	30.00	125.00
1918D	7380	14.00	25.00	60.00	175.00
1918S, All Kinds	11,072	9.00	12.00	30.00	130.00
1918S over 7	—	750.00	1,400.00	3,000.00	8,000.00
1919	11,324	17.00	25.00	40.00	140.00
1919D	1944	30.00	65.00	140.00	450.00
1919S	1836	30.00	60.00	130.00	400.00
1920	27,860	9.00	11.00	25.00	120.00
1920D	3586	15.00	30.00	80.00	200.00
1920S	6380	9.00	15.00	30.00	120.00
1921	1916	35.00	80.00	150.00	375.00
1923	9716	8.00	12.00	25.00	135.00
1923S	1360	60.00	115.00	250.00	550.00
1924	10,920	9.00	12.00	25.00	135.00
1924D	3112	15.00	25.00	60.00	150.00
1924S	2860	10.00	20.00	30.00	150.00
1925	12,280	3.50	6.00	20.00	130.00
1926	11,316	3.50	6.00	20.00	130.00
1926D	1716	3.50	6.00	20.00	130.00
1926S	2700	3.50	6.00	32.00	210.00
1927	11,912	3.50	6.00	20.00	130.00
1927D	976	3.50	8.50	25.00	150.00
1927S	396	5.00	40.00	100.00	1,650.00
1928	6336	3.50	6.00	20.00	130.00
1928D	1628	3.50	6.00	20.00	130.00
1928S	2644	3.50	6.00	20.00	130.00
1929	11,140	3.50	6.00	20.00	130.00
1929D	1358	3.50	6.00	20.00	130.00
1929S	1764	3.50	6.00	20.00	130.00
1930	5632	3.50	6.00	20.00	130.00
1930S	1556	3.50	6.00	20.00	130.00

WASHINGTON HEAD TYPE

	Mintage in Thousands	V.Good	Fine	Ex. Fine	Unc.	Proof
1932	5404	—	—	7.00	30.00	—
1932D	437	40.00	60.00	125.00	650.00	—
1932S	408	40.00	45.00	75.00	350.00	—
1934	31,912	—	—	4.00	20.00	—

	Mintage in Thousands	V. Good	Fine	Ex. Fine	Unc.	Proof
1934D	3527	—	3.50	12.00	125.00	—
1935	32,484	—	—	3.00	20.00	—
1935D	5780	—	3.50	11.00	125.00	—
1935S	5660	—	3.50	10.00	100.00	—
1936	41,304	—	—	3.00	20.00	1,100.00
1936D	5374	2.50	5.00	40.00	280.00	—
1936S	3828	—	3.50	9.00	55.00	—
1937	19,702	—	—	3.00	20.00	500.00
1937D	7190	—	—	8.00	40.00	—
1937S	1652	4.00	7.00	20.00	125.00	—
1938	9480	—	4.00	12.00	70.00	375.00
1938S	2832	—	4.00	10.00	55.00	—
1939	33,549	—	—	3.00	20.00	275.00
1939D	7992	—	—	8.00	35.00	—
1939S	2628	—	4.00	10.00	45.00	—
1940	35,715	—	—	3.50	10.00	150.00
1940D	2798	—	4.00	12.50	60.00	—
1940S	8244	—	—	3.00	30.00	—
1941	79,047	—	—	—	8.00	125.00
1941D	16,715	—	—	—	20.00	—
1941S	16,080	—	—	—	22.00	—
1942	102,117	—	—	—	8.00	115.00
1942D	17,487	—	—	—	15.00	—
1942S	19,384	—	—	—	65.00	—
1943	99,700	—	—	—	7.00	—
1943D	16,096	—	—	—	18.00	—
1943S	21,700	—	—	—	55.00	—
1944	104,956	—	—	—	7.00	—
1944D	14,601	—	—	—	15.00	—
1944S	12,560	—	—	—	18.00	—
1945	74,372	—	—	—	10.00	—
1945D	12,342	—	—	—	10.00	—
1945S	17,004	—	—	—	10.00	—
1946	53,436	—	—	—	7.00	—
1946D	9073	—	—	—	7.00	—
1946S	4204	—	—	—	7.00	—
1947	22,556	—	—	—	8.00	—
1947D	15,338	—	—	—	11.00	—
1947S	5532	—	—	—	9.00	—
1948	35,196	—	—	—	6.00	—
1948D	16,767	—	—	—	6.00	—
1948S	15,960	—	—	—	8.00	—
1949	9312	—	—	—	25.00	—
1949D	10,068	—	—	—	8.00	—
1950	24,972	—	—	—	6.00	90.00
1950D	21,076	—	—	—	6.00	—
1950S	10,284	—	—	—	13.00	—
1951	43,506	—	—	—	5.00	65.00
1951D	35,355	—	—	—	5.00	—
1951S	9048	—	—	—	11.00	—
1952	38,862	—	—	—	5.00	50.00
1952D	49,795	—	—	—	5.00	—
1952S	13,708	—	—	—	9.00	—
1953	18,665	—	—	—	4.00	40.00
1953D	56,112	—	—	—	4.00	—
1953S	14,016	—	—	—	5.00	—
1954	54,646	—	—	—	3.00	25.00
1954D	46,306	—	—	—	3.00	—

	Mintage in Thousands				Unc.	Proof
1954S	11,835	—	—	—	4.00	—
1955	18,558	—	—	—	4.00	20.00
1955D	3182	—	—	—	4.00	—
1956	44,813	—	—	—	3.50	10.00
1956D	32,335	—	—	—	3.50	—
1957	47,780	—	—	—	3.50	5.00
1957D	77,924	—	—	—	3.50	—
1958	7236	—	—	—	3.50	5.00
1958D	78,125	—	—	—	3.50	—
1959	25,533	—	—	—	3.50	5.00
1959D	62,054	—	—	—	3.50	—
1960	30,856	—	—	—	3.50	5.00
1960D	63,000	—	—	—	3.50	—
1961	40,064	—	—	—	3.50	5.00
1961D	83,657	—	—	—	3.50	—
1962	39,374	—	—	—	3.50	5.00
1962D	127,555	—	—	—	3.50	—
1963	77,392	—	—	—	3.50	5.00
1963D	135,288	—	—	—	3.50	—
1964	564,341	—	—	—	3.50	5.00
1964D	704,136	—	—	—	3.50	
1965	1,819,718	—	—	—	—	.50
1966	821,102	—	—	—	—	.50
1967	1,524,032	—	—	—	—	.50
1968	220,732	—	—	—	—	.50
1968D	101,534	—	—	—	—	.50
1968S Proof only	3,042	—	—	—	—	1.00
1969	176,212	—	—	—	—	.50
1969D	114,372	—	—	—	—	.50
1969S Proof only	2,935	—	—	—	—	1.00
1970	136,420	—	—	—	—	.50
1970D	417,341	—	—	—	—	.50
1970S Proof only	2,633	—	—	—	—	1.00
1971	109,284	—	—	—	—	.50
1971D	258,634	—	—	—	—	.50
1971S Proof only	3,224	—	—	—	—	1.00
1972	215,048	—	—	—	—	.50
1972D	311,068	—	—	—	—	.50
1972S Proof only	3,268	—	—	—	—	1.00
1973	346,924	—	—	—	—	.50
1973D	232,977	—	—	—	—	.50
1973S Proof only	2,770	—	—	—	—	1.25
1974	801,456	—	—	—	—	.50
1974D	353,160	—	—	—	—	.50
1974S Proof only	2,617	—	—	—	—	1.00
1976 P-D	725,081	—	—	—	—	.50
1976S Proof only	4,150	—	—	—	—	1.00
1976S Silver Proof	4,000,000	—	—	—	—	2.50
1977S Proof only	3,251	—	—	—	—	1.00
1977 P-D	725,081	—	—	—	—	.50
1978 P-D	808,825	—	—	—	—	.50
1978S Proof only	3,128	—	—	—	—	1.50
1979 P-D	1,005,498	—	—	—	—	.50
1979S Proof only	3,677	—	—	—	—	1.50
1980 P&D	—	—	—	—	—	.50
1980 Proof only	—	—	—	—	—	1.50
1981 P&D	—	—	—	—	—	.50
1981S Proof only	—	—	—	—	—	

(Note: No 1975 dated quarters were minted.)

34.
HALF DOLLARS—
1794–Date

FLOWING HAIR TYPE

	Mintage in Thousands	Good	Fine	V. Fine	Unc.
1794	5	900.00	1,400.00	2,150.00	—
1795	318	700.00	1,100.00	1,900.00	12,500.00

DRAPED BUST TYPE

1796–1797   **1801–1807**

1796 15 Stars, All Kinds	4	10,000.00	20,000.00	30,000.00	—
1796 16 Stars	—	10,000.00	20,000.00	30,000.00	—
1797, All Kinds	4	10,000.00	20,000.00	30,000.00	—
1801	30	100.00	250.00	450.00	7,500.00
1802	30	100.00	250.00	350.00	6,500.00
1803	188	60.00	125.00	200.00	6,000.00
1805 over 4, All Kinds	212	70.00	150.00	300.00	6,000.00
1805	—	60.00	125.00	200.00	6,000.00

	Mintage in Thousands	Good	Fine	V. Fine	Unc.
1806 over 5, All Kinds	840	60.00	125.00	200.00	6,000.00
1806 over inverted 6	—	65.00	125.00	300.00	6,000.00
1806..............................	—	60.00	125.00	200.00	6,000.00
1807..............................	301	60.00	125.00	200.00	6,000.00

TURBAN HEAD TYPE

1807–1836   1836–1839

	Mintage in Thousands	Good	Fine	V. Fine	Unc.
1807, All Kinds	751	25.00	50.00	100.00	600.00
1807 50 over 20.................	—	25.00	40.00	85.00	700.00
1808 over 7, All Kinds	1369	20.00	40.00	60.00	600.00
1808..............................	—	20.00	30.00	50.00	600.00
1809..............................	1406	20.00	30.00	50.00	600.00
1810..............................	1276	20.00	30.00	50.00	600.00
1811..............................	1204	20.00	30.00	50.00	600.00
1812 over 11, All Kinds	1628	20.00	30.00	50.00	600.00
1812..............................	—	20.00	30.00	50.00	600.00
1813..............................	1242	20.00	30.00	50.00	600.00
1814 over 13, All Kinds	1039	20.00	30.00	60.00	600.00
1814..............................	—	20.00	30.00	50.00	600.00
1815 over 12	47	150.00	350.00	500.00	3,000.00
1817 over 13, All Kinds	1216	20.00	45.00	60.00	400.00
1817 over 14 (Rare)	—	—	—	—	—
1817..............................	—	20.00	25.00	35.00	600.00
1818 over 17, All Kinds	1960	20.00	25.00	35.00	600.00
1818..............................	—	20.00	25.00	35.00	600.00
1819 over 18, All Kinds	2208	20.00	25.00	35.00	600.00
1819..............................	—	20.00	25.00	35.00	600.00
1820 over 19, All Kinds	251	20.00	38.00	50.00	600.00
1820..............................	—	20.00	38.00	50.00	600.00
1821..............................	1306	20.00	30.00	50.00	600.00
1822, All Kinds	1560	20.00	30.00	50.00	600.00
1822 over 1	—	40.00	80.00	100.00	600.00
1823 Broken 3, All Kinds.....	1694	40.00	80.00	100.00	600.00
1823..............................	—	20.00	25.00	35.00	600.00
1824 over 21, All Kinds	3505	20.00	30.00	50.00	600.00
1824 over Various Dates	—	20.00	30.00	35.00	600.00
1824..............................	—	20.00	30.00	35.00	600.00
1825..............................	2943	20.00	30.00	35.00	600.00
1826..............................	4004	20.00	30.00	35.00	600.00
1827 over 6, All Kinds	5493	30.00	40.00	60.00	600.00

	Mintage in Thousands	Good	Fine	V. Fine	Unc.
1827	—	20.00	25.00	30.00	600.00
1828	3075	20.00	25.00	30.00	600.00
1829 over 27, All Kinds	—	20.00	25.00	30.00	600.00
1829, All Kinds	3712	20.00	25.00	30.00	600.00
1830	4765	20.00	25.00	30.00	600.00
1831	5874	20.00	25.00	30.00	600.00
1832	4797	20.00	25.00	30.00	600.00
1833	5206	20.00	25.00	30.00	600.00
1834	6412	20.00	25.00	30.00	600.00
1835	5352	20.00	25.00	30.00	600.00
1836 (Lettered edge), All Kinds	6545	20.00	25.00	30.00	600.00
1836 50 over 00	—	30.00	50.00	75.00	600.00
1836 Reeded edge	1	250.00	600.00	900.00	3,750.00
1837	3630	25.00	45.00	70.00	1,400.00
1838	3546	25.00	45.00	70.00	1,400.00
1838O Very Rare	20 Pieces	—	—	—	—
1839	3335	25.00	45.00	70.00	1,400.00
1839O	179	55.00	110.00	125.00	2,150.00

LIBERTY SEATED TYPE

1839–1865   1866–1891

	Mintage in Thousands	Good	Fine	V. Fine	Unc.
1839 No Drapery from Elbow	(included above)	35.00	85.00	140.00	7,500.00
1839 With Drapery	(included above)	10.00	17.00	30.00	650.00
1840	1435	10.00	15.00	25.00	650.00
1840O	855	10.00	15.00	25.00	650.00
1841	310	12.00	24.00	40.00	650.00
1841O	401	10.00	15.00	25.00	650.00
1842	2013	10.00	15.00	25.00	650.00
1842O	957	10.00	15.00	25.00	650.00
1843	3844	10.00	15.00	25.00	650.00
1843O	2268	12.00	30.00	50.00	650.00
1844	1766	10.00	15.00	25.00	650.00
1844O	2005	11.00	22.00	40.00	650.00
1845	589	10.00	15.00	25.00	650.00
1845O, All Kinds	2094	10.00	15.00	25.00	650.00
1845O No Drapery	—	30.00	55.00	100.00	650.00
1846, All Kinds	2210	10.00	15.00	25.00	650.00
1846 over horizontal 6	—	40.00	85.00	135.00	650.00
1846O	2304	10.00	15.00	25.00	650.00
1847 over 46, All Kinds	1156	—	—	—	Rare
1847	—	10.00	15.00	25.00	650.00

	Mintage in Thousands	Good	Fine	V. Fine	Unc.
1847O	2584	10.00	15.00	25.00	650.00
1848................................	580	10.00	15.00	25.00	650.00
1848O	3180	10.00	15.00	25.00	650.00
1849................................	1252	10.00	15.00	25.00	650.00
1849O	2310	10.00	15.00	25.00	650.00
1850................................	227	30.00	50.00	100.00	650.00
1850O	2456	10.00	15.00	25.00	650.00
1851................................	201	30.00	50.00	100.00	650.00
1851O	402	10.00	15.00	25.00	650.00
1852................................	77	40.00	90.00	180.00	850.00
1852O	144	25.00	40.00	100.00	650.00
1853O No Rays & Arrows (Very rare).................	—	—	—	—	—
1853 Arrows & Rays	3533	15.00	35.00	65.00	3,000.00
1853O	1328	15.00	35.00	65.00	3,500.00

	Mintage in Thousands	Good	Fine	V. Fine	Unc.	Proof
1854 Arrows at Date	2982	10.00	20.00	30.00	1,000.00	—
1854O	5240	10.00	20.00	30.00	1,000.00	—
1855.................	760	10.00	20.00	30.00	1,100.00	—
1855 over 54	760	40.00	90.00	225.00	1,500.00	—
1855O	3688	10.00	20.00	30.00	1,100.00	—
1855S.................	130	40.00	110.00	250.00	2,200.00	—
1856 No Arrows ..	938	10.00	20.00	30.00	325.00	—
1856O	2658	10.00	20.00	30.00	650.00	—
1856S.................	211	15.00	40.00	100.00	650.00	—
1857.................	1988	10.00	20.00	30.00	650.00	—
1857O	818	10.00	20.00	30.00	650.00	—
1857S.................	158	15.00	35.00	100.00	650.00	—
1858.................	4226	10.00	20.00	30.00	650.00	1,650.00
1858O	7294	10.00	20.00	30.00	650.00	—
1858S.................	476	15.00	25.00	40.00	650.00	—
1859.................	748	10.00	20.00	30.00	650.00	950.00
1859O	2834	10.00	20.00	30.00	350.00	—
1859S.................	566	12.00	25.00	40.00	650.00	—
1860.................	304	10.00	20.00	30.00	650.00	700.00
1860O	1290	10.00	20.00	30.00	650.00	—
1860S.................	472	15.00	25.00	30.00	650.00	—
1861.................	2888	10.00	20.00	30.00	650.00	700.00
1861O	2533	10.00	20.00	30.00	650.00	—
1861S.................	940	10.00	20.00	30.00	650.00	—
1862.................	254	10.00	20.00	30.00	650.00	700.00
1862S.................	1352	10.00	20.00	30.00	650.00	—
1863.................	504	10.00	20.00	30.00	650.00	700.00
1863S.................	916	10.00	20.00	30.00	650.00	—
1864.................	380	10.00	20.00	30.00	650.00	700.00
1864S.................	658	10.00	20.00	30.00	650.00	—
1865.................	512	10.00	20.00	30.00	650.00	700.00
1865S.................	675	10.00	20.00	30.00	650.00	—
1866 Motto.........	746	10.00	20.00	30.00	650.00	700.00
1866S No Motto, All Kinds.....	1054	40.00	100.00	200.00	4,000.00	—
1866S Motto.......	—	10.00	20.00	30.00	650.00	—
1867.................	450	10.00	20.00	30.00	650.00	700.00
1867S.................	1196	10.00	20.00	30.00	650.00	—
1868.................	418	10.00	20.00	30.00	650.00	700.00

	Mintage in Thousands	Good	Fine	V. Fine	Unc.	Proof
1868S	1160	10.00	20.00	30.00	650.00	—
1869	796	10.00	20.00	30.00	650.00	700.00
1869S	656	10.00	20.00	30.00	650.00	—
1870	635	10.00	20.00	30.00	650.00	700.00
1870CC	55	60.00	175.00	225.00	2,500.00	—
1870S	1004	10.00	20.00	30.00	650.00	—
1871	1205	10.00	20.00	30.00	650.00	700.00
1871CC	140	50.00	100.00	200.00	1,200.00	—
1871S	2178	10.00	20.00	30.00	650.00	—
1872	882	10.00	20.00	30.00	650.00	700.00
1872CC	272	35.00	75.00	125.00	1,000.00	—
1872S	580	10.00	20.00	30.00	650.00	—
1873	802	10.00	20.00	30.00	650.00	700.00
1873CC	123	40.00	100.00	150.00	1,800.00	—
1873 Arrows	1816	15.00	40.00	80.00	1,500.00	2,500.00
1873S	228	25.00	60.00	100.00	1,500.00	—
1873CC	215	30.00	80.00	130.00	2,000.00	—
1874	2360	15.00	40.00	80.00	1,500.00	2,500.00
1874CC	59	40.00	150.00	225.00	2,000.00	—
1874S	394	30.00	70.00	100.00	1,800.00	—
1875 No Arrows	6028	10.00	20.00	30.00	650.00	700.00
1875CC	1008	10.00	20.00	40.00	650.00	—
1875S	3200	10.00	20.00	30.00	650.00	—
1876	8419	10.00	20.00	30.00	650.00	700.00
1876CC	1956	10.00	20.00	30.00	650.00	—
1876S	4528	10.00	20.00	30.00	650.00	—
1877	8305	10.00	20.00	30.00	650.00	700.00
1877CC	1420	10.00	20.00	40.00	650.00	—
1877S	5356	10.00	20.00	30.00	650.00	—
1878	1378	10.00	20.00	30.00	650.00	700.00
1878CC	62	85.00	150.00	250.00	1,200.00	—
1878S	12	800.00	1,500.00	2,000.00	7,500.00	—
1879	6	55.00	70.00	85.00	750.00	800.00
1880	10	50.00	70.00	85.00	750.00	800.00
1881	11	50.00	70.00	85.00	750.00	800.00
1882	6	50.00	70.00	90.00	750.00	800.00
1883	9	50.00	70.00	85.00	750.00	800.00
1884	5	50.00	70.00	85.00	750.00	800.00
1885	6	50.00	70.00	85.00	750.00	800.00
1886	6	75.00	90.00	110.00	750.00	800.00
1887	6	65.00	80.00	100.00	750.00	800.00
1888	13	65.00	80.00	100.00	750.00	800.00
1889	13	65.00	80.00	100.00	750.00	800.00
1890	13	65.00	80.00	100.00	750.00	800.00
1891	201	10.00	20.00	30.00	750.00	800.00

BARBER OR LIBERTY HEAD TYPE

	Mintage in Thousands	Good	Fine	V. Fine	Unc.	Proof
1892	935	7.00	20.00	37.00	650.00	1,100.00
1892O	390	75.00	110.00	180.00	1,400.00	—
1892S	1029	70.00	90.00	150.00	1,200.00	—
1893	1827	9.00	20.00	37.00	750.00	1,100.00
1893O	1389	12.50	30.00	80.00	900.00	—
1893S	740	35.00	65.00	150.00	1,000.00	—
1894	1149	7.00	20.00	37.00	750.00	1,100.00
1894O	2138	7.00	22.00	40.00	800.00	—
1894S	4049	7.00	20.00	40.00	700.00	—
1895	1835	7.00	20.00	37.00	700.00	1,100.00
1895O	1766	7.00	20.00	37.00	950.00	—
1895S	1108	13.00	30.00	52.00	700.00	—
1896	951	7.00	20.00	51.00	700.00	1,100.00
1896O	924	11.00	30.00	52.00	1,750.00	—
1896S	1141	30.00	65.00	90.00	1,750.00	—
1897	2481	7.00	15.00	40.00	650.00	1,100.00
1897O	632	28.00	65.00	90.00	2,100.00	—
1897S	934	60.00	75.00	110.00	1,600.00	—
1898	2957	7.00	15.00	32.00	650.00	1,100.00
1898O	874	7.50	20.00	42.00	900.00	—
1898S	2359	7.00	15.00	40.00	875.00	—
1899	5539	7.00	15.00	32.00	650.00	1,100.00
1899O	1724	7.00	15.00	32.00	1,000.00	—
1899S	1686	7.00	20.00	37.00	800.00	—
1900	4763	7.00	15.00	32.00	650.00	1,100.00
1900O	2744	7.00	15.00	32.00	1,100.00	—
1900S	2560	7.00	15.00	32.00	850.00	—
1901	4269	7.00	15.00	32.00	650.00	1,100.00
1901O	1124	7.00	17.00	42.00	1,450.00	—
1901S	847	10.00	40.00	90.00	1,800.00	—
1902	4923	7.00	15.00	32.00	650.00	1,100.00
1902O	2526	7.00	15.00	32.00	900.00	—
1902S	1461	7.00	15.00	37.00	900.00	—
1903	2279	7.00	15.00	32.00	650.00	1,100.00
1903O	2100	7.00	15.00	32.00	900.00	—
1903S	1921	7.00	15.00	37.00	850.00	—
1904	2993	7.00	15.00	32.00	650.00	1,100.00
1904O	1118	7.00	15.00	37.00	1,500.00	—
1904S	553	10.00	30.00	60.00	1,400.00	—
1905	663	7.00	20.00	42.00	900.00	1,100.00
1905O	505	9.00	28.00	50.00	1,000.00	—
1905S	2494	7.00	15.00	32.00	850.00	—
1906	2639	7.00	15.00	32.00	650.00	1,100.00
1906D	4028	7.00	15.00	32.00	650.00	—

	Mintage in Thousands	Good	Fine	V. Fine	Unc.	Proof
1906O	2446	7.00	15.00	32.00	750.00	—
1906S	1740	7.00	15.00	32.00	800.00	—
1907	2599	7.00	15.00	32.00	650.00	1,100.00
1907D	3856	7.00	15.00	32.00	650.00	—
1907O	3947	7.00	15.00	32.00	700.00	—
1907S	1250	7.00	15.00	32.00	900.00	—
1908	1355	7.00	15.00	32.00	650.00	1,100.00
1908D	3280	7.00	15.00	32.00	650.00	—
1908O	5360	7.00	15.00	32.00	650.00	—
1908S	1645	7.00	15.00	32.00	750.00	—
1909	2369	7.00	15.00	32.00	650.00	1,100.00
1909O	925	7.00	15.00	32.00	1,200.00	—
1909S	1764	7.00	15.00	100.00	800.00	—
1910	419	7.00	18.00	110.00	850.00	1,100.00
1910S	1948	7.00	15.00	90.00	750.00	—
1911	1407	7.00	15.00	90.00	650.00	1,100.00
1911D	695	7.00	15.00	90.00	650.00	—
1911S	1272	7.00	15.00	90.00	700.00	—
1912	1551	7.00	15.00	90.00	650.00	1,100.00
1912D	2301	7.00	15.00	90.00	650.00	—
1912S	1370	7.00	15.00	90.00	700.00	—
1913	189	13.00	30.00	125.00	1,100.00	1,300.00
1913D	534	7.00	15.00	90.00	650.00	—
1913S	604	7.00	15.00	95.00	750.00	—
1914	125	20.00	60.00	135.00	1,200.00	1,800.00
1914S	992	7.00	15.00	90.00	750.00	—
1915	138	18.00	40.00	115.00	1,150.00	1,500.00
1915D	1170	7.00	15.00	90.00	650.00	—
1915S	1604	7.00	15.00	90.00	650.00	—

LIBERTY WALKING TYPE

	Mintage in Thousands	Good	Fine	Ex. Fine	Unc.
1916	608	15.00	35.00	150.00	450.00
1916D on Obverse	1014	10.00	15.00	100.00	400.00
1916S on Obverse	508	20.00	60.00	250.00	1,000.00
1917	12,292	7.00	11.00	25.00	150.00
1917D on Obverse	765	7.00	20.00	90.00	450.00
1917D on Reverse	1940	7.00	11.00	80.00	550.00
1917S on Obverse	952	10.00	20.00	200.00	1,200.00
1917S on Reverse	5554	7.00	11.00	30.00	275.00
1918	6634	7.00	11.00	80.00	350.00
1918D	3853	7.00	11.00	85.00	900.00

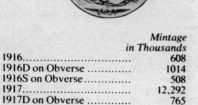

	Mintage in Thousands	Good	Fine	Ex. Fine	Unc.
1918S	10,282	6.50	7.50	27.00	250.00
1919	962	6.50	15.00	200.00	1,200.00
1919D	1165	6.50	14.00	250.00	2,500.00
1919S	1552	6.50	12.00	200.00	2,300.00
1920	6372	6.50	7.50	28.00	225.00
1920D	1551	6.50	9.00	150.00	1,500.00
1920S	4624	6.50	8.00	60.00	1,200.00
1921	246	40.00	110.00	700.00	2,500.00
1921D	208	60.00	150.00	900.00	2,800.00
1921S	548	12.00	30.00	950.00	11,000.00
1923S	2178	6.50	10.00	90.00	1,100.00
1927S	2392	6.50	10.00	50.00	900.00
1928S	1940	6.50	10.00	80.00	1,000.00
1929D	1001	6.50	10.00	50.00	350.00
1929S	1902	6.50	7.50	40.00	350.00
1933S	1786	6.50	7.50	15.00	350.00
1934	6964	—	7.50	10.00	120.00
1934D	2361	—	7.50	15.00	240.00
1934S	3652	—	7.50	20.00	450.00
1935	9162	—	7.50	100.00	70.00
1935D	3004	—	7.50	15.00	220.00
1935S	3854	—	7.50	22.00	350.00

	Mintage in Thousands	Good	Fine	Ex. Fine	Unc.	Proof
1936	12,618	—	7.50	10.00	70.00	2,000.00
1936D	4252	—	7.50	20.00	170.00	—
1936S	3884	—	7.50	20.00	200.00	—
1937	9528	—	7.50	10.00	70.00	1,400.00
1937D	1676	—	7.50	30.00	235.00	—
1937S	2090	—	7.50	25.00	230.00	—
1938	4118	—	7.50	12.00	120.00	900.00
1938D	492	20.00	30.00	65.00	600.00	—
1939	6821	—	7.50	10.00	80.00	700.00
1939D	4268	—	7.50	10.00	90.00	—
1939S	2552	—	7.50	15.00	160.00	—
1940	9167	—	—	10.00	50.00	350.00
1940S	4550	—	—	10.00	120.00	—
1941	24,207	—	—	10.00	30.00	250.00
1941D	11,248	—	—	10.00	70.00	—
1941S	8098	—	—	10.00	180.00	—
1942	47,839	—	—	10.00	30.00	250.00
1942D	10,974	—	—	10.00	70.00	—
1942S	12,708	—	—	10.00	150.00	—

	Mintage in Thousands	Good	Fine	Ex. Fine	Unc.
1943	53,190	—	—	10.00	30.00
1943D	11,346	—	—	10.00	80.00
1943S	13,450	—	—	10.00	130.00
1944	28,206	—	—	10.00	30.00
1944D	9769	—	—	10.00	70.00
1944S	9904	—	—	10.00	120.00
1945	31,502	—	—	10.00	30.00
1945D	9967	—	—	10.00	60.00
1945S	10,156	—	—	10.00	120.00
1946	12,118	—	—	10.00	40.00
1946D	2151	—	—	10.00	70.00

	Mintage in Thousands	Good	Fine	Ex. Fine	Unc.
1946S	3724	—	—	10.00	120.00
1947	4094	—	—	10.00	75.00
1947D	3901	—	—	10.00	65.00

FRANKLIN TYPE

	Mintage in Thousands	Ex. Fine	Unc.	Proof
1948	3007	6.50	25.00	—
1948D	4029	6.50	15.00	—
1949	5614	6.50	80.00	—
1949D	4121	6.50	75.00	—
1949S	3748	6.50	250.00	—
1950	7794	6.50	40.00	275.00
1950D	8032	6.50	30.00	—
1951	16,860	6.50	15.00	175.00
1951D	9475	6.50	65.00	—
1951S	13,696	6.50	30.00	—
1952	21,274	6.50	15.00	100.00
1952D	25,396	6.50	15.00	—
1952S	5526	6.50	35.00	—
1953	2797	6.50	20.00	75.00
1953D	20,900	6.50	10.00	—
1953S	4148	6.50	15.00	—
1954	13,422	6.50	10.00	35.00
1954D	25,446	6.50	10.00	—
1954S	4993	6.50	12.00	—
1955	2876	6.50	15.00	35.00
1956	4701	6.50	13.00	15.00
1957	6362	6.50	10.00	10.00
1957D	19,967	6.50	10.00	—
1958	4918	6.50	10.00	9.00
1958D	23,962	6.50	10.00	—
1959	7349	6.50	10.00	9.00
1959D	13,054	6.50	10.00	—
1960	7716	6.50	10.00	9.00
1960D	18,216	6.50	10.00	—
1961	11,318	6.50	10.00	9.00
1961D	20,276	6.50	10.00	—
1962	12,932	6.50	10.00	9.00
1962D	35,473	6.50	10.00	—
1963	25,240	6.50	10.00	9.00
1963D	67,069	6.50	10.00	—

KENNEDY TYPE

	Mintage in Thousands	Unc.	Proof
1964...	277,255	7.00	8.00
1964D	156,205	7.50	—
1965...	65,879	3.00	—
1966...	108,985	3.00	—
1967...	295,047	3.00	—
1968D	246,952	3.00	—
1968S Proof only	3042	—	5.00
1969D	129,882	3.00	—
1969S Proof only	2935	—	5.00
1970D	2150	40.00	—
1970S Proof Only	2633	—	15.00

		Unc.	Unc.
1971...	155,164	—	.90
1971D..	302,097	—	.90
1971S Proof only	3,224	--	4.00
1972...	153,180	—	.90
1972D..	141,890	—	.90
1972S Proof only	3,268	—	4.00
1973...	64,964	—	1.00
1973D..	83,171	—	1.00
1973S Proof only	2,770	—	5.00
1974...	201,596	—	1.00
1974D..	79,066	—	1.00
1974S Proof only	2,617	—	4.00
1976 P-D..	521,873	—	1.00
1976S Proof only	7,059	—	2.00
1976S Silver Proof	4,000,000	—	7.00
1977 P-D..	75,047	—	1.00
1977S Proof only	3,251	—	3.00
1978 P-D..	28,116	—	1.00
1978S Proof only	3,128	—	7.00
1979 P-D..	84,127	—	1.00
1979S Proof only	—	—	5.00
1980 P-D..	—	—	1.00
1980S Proof only	—	—	5.00
1981 P-D..	—	—	1.00
1981S Proof only	—	—	5.00

35.
SILVER DOLLARS—
1794–1935

FLOWING HAIR TYPE

	Mintage in Thousands	Good	Fine	V. Fine	Unc.
1794............................	2	2,500.00	7,500.00	12,500.00	100,000
1795............................	160	1,500.00	2,200.00	3,200.00	25,000.00

DRAPED BUST TYPE

1795–1798   1798–1804

		Good	Fine	V. Fine	Unc.
1795............................	43	1,400.00	1,800.00	2,500.00	15,000.00
1796............................	73	1,400.00	1,800.00	2,500.00	15,000.00

	Mintage in Thousands	Good	Fine	V. Fine	Unc.
1797 9 Stars Left, 7 Right, All Kinds	8	650.00	800.00	1,400.00	15,000.00
1797 10 Stars Left, 6 Right ...	—	650.00	800.00	1,400.00	15,000.00
1798 13 Stars, All Kinds	328	325.00	650.00	800.00	8,000.00
1798 15 Stars	—	325.00	650.00	800.00	8,000.00
1798 Large eagle................	—	325.00	650.00	800.00	8,000.00
1799 over 98, All Kinds	424	325.00	650.00	800.00	8,000.00
1799 Stars 7 Left, 6 Right, All Kinds	424	325.00	650.00	800.00	8,000.00
1799 Stars 8 Left, 5 Right, All Kinds	424	325.00	650.00	800.00	8,000.00
1800...............................	221	325.00	650.00	800.00	8,000.00
1801...............................	54	325.00	650.00	800.00	8,000.00
1802 over 1, All Kinds	42	325.00	650.00	800.00	8,000.00
1802, All Kinds ..,.............	42	325.00	650.00	800.00	8,000.00
1803...............................	86	325.00	650.00	800.00	8,000.00
1804 Very rare	—	—	—	—	—

GOBRECHT PATTERNS

	Mintage in Thousands	Proof
1836 C. Gobrecht F. in field below base. Reverse Eagle in field of stars (Rare)	1	—
1836 Obverse as above Reverse. Eagle flying in plain field (Rare)	1	—

	Mintage in Thousands	V. Fine	Proof	
				—
1836 C. Gobrecht on base	(inc. above)	1,800.00	4,500.00	—
1838..	about 100 Pieces	—	7,000.00	—
1839..	about 300 Pieces	—	6,500.00	—

LIBERTY SEATED TYPE

1840–1865   1866–1873

	Mintage in Thousands	Good	Fine	Unc.	Proof
1840	61	65.00	95.00	900.00	2,200.00
1841	173	50.00	85.00	900.00	2,000.00
1842	185	50.00	85.00	900.00	2,000.00
1843	165	50.00	85.00	900.00	2,000.00
1844	20	60.00	110.00	900.00	2,200.00
1845	25	60.00	110.00	900.00	2,300.00
1846	111	50.00	85.00	900.00	2,100.00
1846O	59	55.00	85.00	1,500.00	—
1847	141	50.00	85.00	900.00	2,000.00
1848	15	65.00	110.00	900.00	2,100.00
1849	63	55.00	85.00	900.00	2,000.00
1850	8	90.00	140.00	1,150.00	2,400.00
1850O	40	55.00	85.00	950.00	—
1851	1	—	1,000.00	5,500.00	5,000.00
1852	1	—	1,000.00	5,000.00	4,000.00
1853	46	65.00	95.00	950.00	3,500.00
1854	33	70.00	140.00	1,100.00	3,500.00
1855	26	90.00	165.00	1,200.00	3,500.00
1856	64	65.00	115.00	900.00	2,750.00
1857	94	60.00	95.00	900.00	2,500.00
1858	about 80 Pieces	—	—	4,000.00	
1859	257	50.00	85.00	900.00	2,000.00
1859O	360	50.00	85.00	900.00	—
1859S	20	95.00	125.00	950.00	—
1860	219	50.00	85.00	900.00	2,000.00
1860O	515	50.00	85.00	900.00	—
1861	79	65.00	90.00	900.00	2,000.00
1862	12	65.00	90.00	900.00	2,000.00
1863	28	65.00	90.00	900.00	2,000.00
1864	31	65.00	90.00	900.00	2,000.00
1865	47	65.00	90.00	900.00	2,000.00
1866	50	65.00	90.00	900.00	2,000.00
1867	48	65.00	90.00	900.00	2,000.00
1868	163	50.00	85.00	900.00	2,000.00
1869	424	50.00	85.00	900.00	2,000.00

	Mintage in Thousands	Good	Fine	Unc.	Proof
1870	416	50.00	85.00	900.00	1,750.00
1870CC	12	90.00	135.00	1,000.00	—
1870S (Rare)	—	—	—	—	—
1871	1075	50.00	85.00	900.00	1,750.00
1871CC	1	450.00	650.00	4,000.00	—
1872	1106	50.00	85.00	900.00	1,750.00
1872CC	3	200.00	350.00	3,000.00	—
1872S	9	100.00	125.00	1,000.00	—
1873	294	50.00	85.00	900.00	1,750.00
1873CC	2	500.00	1,000.00	6,500.00	—
1873S (unknown)	1	—	—	—	—

MORGAN OR LIBERTY HEAD TYPE

	Mintage in Thousands	Ex. Fine	Unc.	Proof
1878 8 Tail Feathers	750	25.00	50.00	1,700.00
1878 7 Tail Feathers over 8 Tail Feathers, All Kinds	9760	30.00	65.00	—
1878 7 Tail Feathers	—	18.00	45.00	2,000.00
1878CC	2212	30.00	80.00	—
1878S	9774	18.00	35.00	—
1879	14,807	18.00	40.00	1,300.00
1879CC	756	160.00	750.00	—
1879O	2887	18.00	50.00	—
1879S	9110	18.00	35.00	—
1880	12,601	18.00	40.00	1,300.00
1880CC	591	65.00	180.00	—
1880O	5305	18.00	70.00	—
1880S	8900	18.00	35.00	—
1881	9164	18.00	40.00	1,300.00
1881CC	296	75.00	175.00	—
1881O	5708	18.00	35.00	—
1881S	12,760	18.00	35.00	—
1882	11,101	18.00	40.00	1,300.00
1882CC	1133	30.00	75.00	—
1882O	6090	18.00	35.00	—
1882S	9250	18.00	35.00	—
1883	12,291	18.00	40.00	1,300.00
1883CC	1204	30.00	60.00	—
1883O	8725	18.00	30.00	—
1883S	6250	25.00	350.00	—

	Mintage in Thousands	Ex. Fine	Unc.	Proof
1884	14,071	18.00	55.00	1,300.00
1884CC	1136	35.00	65.00	—
1884O	9730	18.00	30.00	—
1884S	3200	25.00	900.00	—
1885	17,788	18.00	30.00	1,300.00
1885CC	228	160.00	165.00	—
1885O	9185	18.00	30.00	—
1885S	1497	22.00	115.00	—
1886	19,964	18.00	30.00	1,300.00
1886O	10,710	18.00	400.00	—
1886S	750	32.00	200.00	—
1887	20,291	18.00	30.00	1,300.00
1887O	11,550	18.00	35.00	—
1887S	1771	18.00	95.00	—
1888	19,184	18.00	30.00	1,300.00
1888O	12,150	18.00	40.00	—
1888S	657	40.00	200.00	—
1889	21,737	18.00	35.00	1,300.00
1889CC	350	550.00	5,500.00	—
1889O	11,875	18.00	100.00	—
1889S	700	35.00	125.00	—
1890	16,803	18.00	40.00	1,300.00
1890CC	2309	30.00	150.00	—
1890O	10,701	18.00	70.00	—
1890S	8230	18.00	55.00	—
1891	8694	18.00	125.00	1,300.00
1891CC	1608	30.00	125.00	—
1891O	7955	18.00	135.00	—
1891S	5296	18.00	65.00	—
1892	1037	18.00	160.00	1,300.00
1892CC	1352	55.00	250.00	—
1892O	2742	18.00	180.00	—
1892S	1200	140.00	5,000.00	—
1893	379	80.00	425.00	1,700.00
1893CC	677	235.00	900.00	—
1893O	300	225.00	950.00	—
1893S	100	3,150.00	20,000.00	—
1894	111	450.00	1,100.00	2,500.00
1894O	1723	25.00	450.00	—
1894S	1260	70.00	380.00	—
1895	13	—	—	12,000.00
1895O	450	225.00	2,400.00	—
1895S	400	350.00	1,300.00	—
1896	9977	18.00	35.00	1,300.00
1896O	4900	18.00	650.00	—
1896S	5000	70.00	635.00	—
1897	2823	18.00	45.00	1,300.00
1897O	4004	18.00	450.00	—
1897S	5825	18.00	65.00	—
1898	5885	18.00	40.00	1,300.00
1898O	4440	18.00	30.00	—
1898S	4102	18.00	240.00	—
1899	331	50.00	90.00	1,300.00
1899O	12,290	18.00	30.00	—
1899S	2562	25.00	325.00	—
1900	8831	18.00	30.00	1,300.00
1900O	12,590	18.00	30.00	—
1900S	3540	18.00	210.00	—

	Mintage in Thousands	Ex. Fine	Unc.	Proof
1901	6963	35.00	800.00	2,100.00
1901O	13,320	18.00	35.00	—
1901S	2284	25.00	325.00	—
1902	7995	18.00	55.00	1,300.00
1902O	8636	18.00	30.00	—
1902S	1530	70.00	350.00	—
1903	4653	18.00	60.00	1,300.00
1903O	4450	250.00	290.00	—
1903S	1241	125.00	2,200.00	—
1904	2789	18.00	250.00	1,300.00
1904O	3720	18.00	30.00	—
1904S	2304	90.00	1,200.00	—
1921	44,690	18.00	22.00	—
1921D	20,345	18.00	32.00	—
1921S	21,695	18.00	48.00	—

PEACE TYPE

	Mintage in Thousands	Ex. Fine	Unc.	Proof
1921	1006	60.00	650.00	—
1922	51,737	16.00	20.00	—
1922D	15,063	16.00	45.00	—
1922S	17,475	16.00	48.00	—
1923	30,800	16.00	20.00	—
1923D	6811	16.00	45.00	—
1923S	13,020	16.00	70.00	—
1924	11,811	16.00	27.00	—
1924S	1728	25.00	210.00	—
1925	10,198	16.00	23.00	—
1925S	1610	20.00	180.00	—
1926	1939	16.00	45.00	—
1926D	2349	20.00	110.00	—
1926S	6980	16.00	50.00	—
1927	848	25.00	95.00	—
1927D	1269	25.00	250.00	—
1927S	866	21.00	310.00	—

	Mintage in Thousands	Ex. Fine	Unc.	Proof
1928	361	150.00	275.00	—
1928S	1632	20.00	210.00	—
1934	954	22.00	140.00	—
1934D	1570	20.00	130.00	—
1934S	1011	135.00	2,150.00	—
1935	1576	20.00	70.00	—
1935S	1964	20.00	180.00	—

EISENHOWER DOLLAR

	Mintage in Thousands	Unc.	Proof
1971 Copper Nickel	47,799	2.00	—
1971D Copper Nickel	68,587	2.50	—
1971S Silver	11,134	6.00	7.00
1972 Copper Nickel	75,890	2.00	—
1972D Copper Nickel	92,549	2.50	—
1972S Silver	4,005	12.00	20.00
1973 Copper Nickel	2,000	13.00	—
1973D Copper Nickel	2,000	13.00	—
1973S Copper Nickel	2,770	—	9.00
1973S Silver	2,889	15.00	90.00
1974 Copper Nickel	27,366	1.50	—
1974D Copper Nickel	45,517	1.50	—
1974S Copper Nickel	2,617	—	6.00
1974S Silver	3,215	12.00	30.00
1976 Copper Nickel	117,338	1.50	—
1976D Copper Nickel	103,228	1.50	—
1976S Silver	15,000	8.00	10.00
1976S Copper Nickel	6,995	—	4.00
1977 Copper Nickel	12,596	2.50	—
1977D Copper Nickel	32,983	2.50	—
1977S Copper Nickel	3,251	—	4.00
Note: No 1975 dated dollars were struck.			
1978	25,702	1.50	—
1978D	23,013	1.50	—
1978-S Copper Nickel	3,128	—	12.00
ANTHONY DOLLARS			
1979 P	—	1.50	—
1979 D	—	1.50	—
1979S	—	1.50	—
1980P	—	1.50	11.00
1980D	—	1.50	—
1980S	—	5.00	11.00

36.
TRADE DOLLARS—
1873–1885

	Mintage in Thousands	V. Good	Fine	Ex. Fine	Unc.	Proof
1873.................	398	50.00	55.00	85.00	600.00	2,250.00
1873CC	125	55.00	65.00	145.00	700.00	—
1873S	703	50.00	55.00	90.00	650.00	—
1874.................	988	50.00	55.00	85.00	600.00	2,250.00
1874CC	1373	55.00	65.00	100.00	650.00	—
1874S	2549	50.00	55.00	85.00	600.00	—
1875.................	219	75.00	95.00	180.00	950.00	2,250.00
1875CC	1574	60.00	70.00	100.00	750.00	—
1875S	4487	50.00	55.00	80.00	600.00	—
1876.................	456	50.00	55.00	80.00	600.00	2,250.00
1876CC	509	60.00	65.00	115.00	750.00	—
1876S	5227	50.00	55.00	80.00	600.00	—
1877.................	3040	50.00	55.00	80.00	600.00	2,250.00
1877CC	534	70.00	80.00	150.00	900.00	—
1877S	9519	50.00	55.00	80.00	600.00	—
1878.................	1	—	—	—	—	2,850.00
1878CC	97	125.00	250.00	450.00	2,300.00	—
1878S	4162	50.00	55.00	80.00	600.00	—
1879.................	2	—	—	—	—	2,500.00
1880.................	2	—	—	—	—	2,500.00
1881.................	1	—	—	—	—	3,000.00
1882.................	1	—	—	—	—	3,000.00
1883.................	1	—	—	—	—	3,350.00
1884 Only 10 Struck.........	—	—	—	—	—	40,000.00
1885 Only 5 Struck.........	—	—	—	—	—	90,000.00

(Note: Trade dollars with oriental counterstamps ("Gin" marks) are worth considerably less than quoted values.)

37.
SILVER COMMEMORATIVE COINS
(Half Dollars unless otherwise specified)

Year	Mintage in Thousands	Ex. Fine	Unc.
1892 Columbian Exposition	950	8.00	18.00
1893 Columbian Exposition	1550	7.00	15.00
1893 Isabella Quarter	24	120.00	375.00
1900 Lafayette Dollar	36	250.00	1,050.00
1915 S Panama-Pacific Exposition	27	125.00	650.00
1918 Illinois Centennial	100	23.00	60.00
1920 Maine Centennial	50	30.00	80.00
1920 Pilgrim Tercentenary	152	20.00	45.00
1921 Pilgrim Tercentenary (1921) on obverse	20	40.00	125.00
1921 Missouri Centennial (with star)	5	165.00	550.00
1921 Missouri Centennial (no star)	15	150.00	525.00
1921 Alabama Centennial (with 2 x 2)	6	70.00	360.00
1921 Alabama Centennial (no 2 x 2)	59	45.00	275.00
1922 Grant Memorial (with star)	4	250.00	550.00
1922 Grant Memorial (no star)	67	24.00	75.00
1923 S Monroe Doctrine Centennial	274	15.00	40.00
1924 Huguenot-Walloon Tercentenary	142	32.00	75.00
1925 Lexington-Concord Sesquicentennial	162	24.00	55.00
1925 Stone Mountain Memorial	1315	12.00	25.00
1925 S California Diamond Jubilee	87	40.00	120.00
1925 Fort Vancouver Centennial	15	130.00	425.00
1926 Sesquicentennial of American Independence	141	15.00	40.00
1926 Oregon Trail Memorial	48	34.00	90.00
1926 Oregon Trail Memorial, S Mint	83	34.00	90.00
1928 Oregon Trail Memorial	6	80.00	200.00
1933 D Oregon Trail Memorial	5	70.00	220.00
1934D Oregon Trail Memorial	7	44.00	160.00
1936 Oregon Trail Memorial	10	34.00	100.00
1936 S Oregon Trail Memorial	5	45.00	150.00
1937 D Oregon Trail Memorial	12	34.00	100.00
1938 P-D-S Oregon Trail Memorial (set of three)	Each 6	90.00	400.00
1939 P-D-S Oregon Trail Memorial (set of three)	Each 3	150.00	650.00
1927 Vermont Sesquicentennial	28	55.00	200.00
1928 Hawaiian Sesquicentennial	10	500.00	1,100.00
1934 Maryland Tercentenary	25	55.00	130.00
1934 Texas Centennial	61	28.00	65.00
1935 P-D-S Texas Centennial (set of three)	Each 10	75.00	190.00
1936 P-D-S Texas Centennial (set of three)	Each 9	75.00	190.00
1937 P-D-S Texas Centennial (set of three)	Each 7	90.00	240.00
1938 P-D-S Texas Centennial (set of three)	Each 4	135.00	450.00
1934 Daniel Boone Bicentennial	10	35.00	80.00
1935 P-D-S Daniel Boone Bicentennial (set of three)	Each 5	75.00	200.00
1935 P-D-S Daniel Boone Bicentennial (set of three)*	Each 2	350.00	1,100.00

Year	Mintage in Thousands	Ex. Fine	Unc.
1936 P-D-S Daniel Boone Bicentennial (set of three)..	Each 5	80.00	200.00
1937 P-D-S Daniel Boone Bicentennial (set of three)..	Each 3	120.00	500.00
1938 P-D-S Daniel Boone Bicentennial (set of three)..	Each 2	225.00	1,000.00
1935 Connecticut Tercentenary	25	80.00	175.00
1935 P-D-S Arkansas Centennial (set of three)	Each 6	70.00	170.00
1936 P-D-S Arkansas Centennial (set of three)	Each 10	65.00	200.00
1937 P-D-S Arkansas Centennial (set of three)	Each 6	65.00	275.00
1938 P-D-S Arkansas Centennial (set of three)	Each 3	100.00	375.00
1939 P-D-S Arkansas Centennial (set of three)	Each 2	250.00	1,000.00
1935 Hudson, N.Y. Sesquicentennial................	10	300.00	550.00
1935 S California-Pacific Exposition	70	25.00	50.00
1936 D California-Pacific Exposition.................	30	25.00	85.00
1935 Old Spanish Trail.....................................	10	400.00	700.00
1936 P-D-S Rhode Island Tercentenary (set of three)..	Each 15	80.00	400.00
1936 Cleveland, Great Lakes Exposition	56	20.00	55.00
1936 Wisconsin Territorial Centennial...............	25	55.00	120.00
1936 P-D-S Cincinnati Musical Center (set of three)..	Each 5	425.00	1,150.00
1936 Long Island Tercentenary.........................	82	25.00	55.00
1936 York County, Maine Tercentenary	25	55.00	120.00
1936 Bridgeport, Conn. Centennial...................	25	40.00	110.00
1936 Lynchburg, Va. Sesquicentennial..............	20	60.00	150.00
1936 Elgin, Illinois Centennial	20	60.00	150.00
1936 Albany, N.Y. Charter	18	90.00	220.00
1936 S San Francisco-Oakland Bay Bridge.........	71	35.00	70.00
1936 P-D-S Columbia, S.C. Sesquicentennial (set of three)..	Each 8	240.00	800.00
1936 Arkansas Centennial-Robinson.................	25	45.00	100.00
1936 Delaware Tercentenary............................	21	75.00	180.00
1936 Battle of Gettysburg (1863-1938)	27	75.00	225.00
1936 Norfolk, Va. Bicentennial	17	120.00	280.00
1937 Roanoke Island, N.C. (1587-1937)	29	45.00	120.00
1937 Battle of Antietam (1862-1937)..................	18	120.00	275.00
1938 New Rochelle, N.Y. (1688-1938)	15	125.00	275.00
1946 Iowa Centennial	100	25.00	60.00

	Mintage in Thousands	Fine	Ex. Fine	Unc.
1946 Booker T. Washington Memorial (set of three).............................	+1001	—	20.00	35.00
1947 Booker T. Washington Memorial (set of three).............................	Each 100	—	30.00	45.00
1948 Booker T. Washington Memorial (set of three).............................	Each 8	—	50.00	70.00
1949 Booker T. Washington Memorial (set of three).............................	Each 6	—	70.00	140.00
1950 Booker T. Washington Memorial (set of three).............................	Each 6 +	—	65.00	140.00
1951 Booker T. Washington Memorial (set of three).............................	Each 7 +	—	50.00	90.00
1951 Washington Carver (set of three).	Each 10	—	30.00	45.00
1952 Washington Carver (set of three).	Each 8	—	30.00	70.00
1953 Washington Carver (set of three).	Each 8	—	40.00	110.00
1954 Washington Carver (set of three).	Each 12	—	30.00	55.00

*Small ''1934'' added on Reverse.

+Additional quantities struck, beyond sets of 3.

38.
GOLD COMMEMORATIVE COINS
(Dollar unless otherwise specified)

Year	Mintage in Thousands	Ex. Fine	Unc.
1903 Louisiana Purchase (Jefferson)	18	250.00	700.00
1903 Louisiana Purchase (McKinley)	18	250.00	700.00
1904 Lewis and Clark Exposition	10	450.00	1,800.00
1905 Lewis and Clark Exposition	10	450.00	1,800.00
1915 S Panama-Pacific Exposition	15	250.00	900.00
1915 S Panama-Pacific Exposition ($2.50)	7	700.00	2,750.00
1915 S Panama-Pacific Exposition ($50 round)	483 Pieces	20,000.00	36,000.00
1915 S Panama-Pacific Exposition ($50 octagonal)	645 Pieces	13,000.00	27,500.00
1916 McKinley Memorial	10	250.00	700.00
1917 McKinley Memorial	10	250.00	750.00
1922 Grant Memorial (with star)	5	500.00	1,500.00
1922 Grant Memorial (no star)	5	500.00	1,500.00
1926 Philadelphia Sesquicentennial ($2.50)	46	250.00	500.00

39.

PROOF SETS

EACH SET CONTAINS A HALF, QUARTER, DIME,
NICKEL AND CENT, SPECIALLY STRUCK AT THE
MINT WITH MIRROR-LIKE FINISH
(ALSO A DOLLAR FROM 1973 ONWARDS)

Date and Number of Sets Coined	Proof
1936 (3,837)	6,500.00
1937 (5,542)	3,800.00
1938 (8,045)	1,700.00
1939 (8,795)	1,300.00
1940 (11,246)	1,100.00
1941 (15,287)	950.00
1942 (21,120) 6 pieces	1,150.00
1950 (51,386)	450.00
1951 (57,500)	300.00
1952 (81,980)	150.00
1953 (128,800)	100.00
1954 (233,300)	65.00
1955 (378,200)	50.00
1956 (669,384)	25.00
1957 (1,247,952)	18.00
1958 (875,652)	23.00
1959 (1,149,291)	18.00
1960 (1,691,602)	14.00
1960 with sm. dt. ct	35.00
1961 (3,028,244)	15.00
1962 (3,218,039)	15.00
1963 (3,075,645)	15.00
1964 (3,950,962)	15.00
1968S (3,041,509)	6.00
1969S (2,934,631)	6.00
1970S (2,632,810)	15.00
1971S (3,224,138)	6.00
1972S (3,267,667)	6.00
1973S (2,769,624)	12.00
1974S (2,617,350)	12.00
1975S (2,909,369)	18.00
1976S (4,149,730)	8.00
1977S (3,251,152)	9.00
1978S (3,127,781)	18.00
1979S Type I	20.00
1979S Type II (each mintmark is sharp and well defined) (3,677,175)	150.00
1980S (approx. 4,000,000)	20.00
1981S	20.00

40.

GOLD, GOLD, THAT MAGIC WORD.

Since the dawn of civilization, gold has been hunted by man!
Treasured beyond belief, its beautiful color, durability, ease of
transportation and scarcity have led man to go to unbelieveable
lengths to secure it. Its demand made it the first basic com-
modity in trade. Ancient Egyptians cherished it, King Croesus
first struck coins out of it, Greeks and Romans buried their
hoards of it in earthen Jars. The Incas in South America
hoarded it, erected statues and made idols out of it. Man
throughout all parts of the world sought it.

In ancient times, armies sacked cities for gold and other
treasures. During the middle ages, walled castles were built
to protect such valuables. Vikings sacked England, Pirates
roved the seas, outlaws robbed, Spain conquered and pilfered
Central and South America. All for gold and treasures.

The discovery of gold in 1849 in California hastened the
population of the far west, caused murders, stage coach and
train robberies. All in the name of the magic word GOLD.

Up until 1933, we had been on the gold standard with the
price of gold set by government edict at about $20 per ounce. A
twenty dollar gold piece contained nearly one ounce of gold,
(with of course some alloy to harden the coin for circulation).
When the dollar was devalued in 1933 the price of a twenty

dollar gold piece immediately was set at $35. This price gradually increased through the years until it reached the $60 figure.

The recent lowering of the value of the dollar again has caused an unbelievable boom in gold prices. Is this the top? Will it go higher? That is the question.

Lets analyze the situation. The currencies of the world, always under the pressure of inflation have been subjected to various degrees of inflation, reducing their purchasing power. There has to be some basic medium by which valuations can be determined. Gold has always been accepted as this medium. This would make gold rise in value. Now, the population of the world is much greater than it ever was, hence we have more demand for gold, but gold supply is limited. Another reason why gold should rise in value.

How high will gold go? Who knows, but it will be determined by the rate of inflation of currencies and demand; today demand is high.

41.
GOLD DOLLARS—
1849–1889

LIBERTY HEAD TYPE

	Mintage in Thousands	V. Fine	Unc.	—
1849	689	250.00	700.00	—
1849C	12	350.00	2,200.00	—
1849D	22	300.00	1,100.00	—
1849O	215	250.00	700.00	—
1850	482	250.00	700.00	—
1850C	7	350.00	1,900.00	—
1850D	8	300.00	1,500.00	—
1850O	14	250.00	700.00	—
1851	3318	250.00	700.00	—
1851C	41	275.00	1,000.00	—
1851D	10	250.00	1,200.00	—
1851O	290	250.00	700.00	—
1852	2045	250.00	700.00	—
1852C	9	300.00	1,250.00	—
1852D	6	250.00	1,750.00	—
1852O	140	250.00	700.00	—
1853	4076	250.00	700.00	—
1853C	12	300.00	1,300.00	—
1853D	7	300.00	1,550.00	—
1853O	290	250.00	700.00	—
1854 Small Planchet	737	250.00	700.00	—
1854D	3	450.00	4,000.00	—
1854S	15	250.00	1,000.00	—

INDIAN HEADDRESS TYPE

	Mintage in Thousands	V. Fine	Unc.	Proof
1854 Large Planchet	903	400.00	3,800.00	—
1855	758	400.00	3,800.00	—
1855C	10	800.00	8,000.00	—
1855D	2	3,000.00	20,000.00	—
1855O	55	600.00	8,500.00	—
1856S	25	450.00	9,000.00	—

LARGER INDIAN HEADDRESS TYPE

	Mintage in Thousands	V. Fine	Unc.	Proof
1856	1763	200.00	650.00	2,200.00
1856D	1	2,500.00	7,000.00	—
1857	775	200.00	650.00	2,400.00
1857C	13	300.00	1,000.00	—
1857D	4	600.00	1,500.00	—
1857S	10	300.00	1,400.00	—
1858	118	200.00	650.00	2,100.00
1858D	3	750.00	2,000.00	—
1858S	10	200.00	1,250.00	—
1859	168	200.00	650.00	2,000.00
1859C	5	350.00	1,100.00	—
1859D	5	325.00	1,600.00	—
1859S	15	200.00	1,150.00	—
1860	37	200.00	650.00	1,400.00
1860D	2	3,500.00	9,000.00	—
1860S	13	200.00	800.00	—
1861	527	200.00	650.00	1,250.00
1861D	—	5,000.00	15,000.00	—
1862	1361	200.00	650.00	2,250.00
1863	6	300.00	1,500.00	3,000.00
1864	6	250.00	1,000.00	2,800.00
1865	4	300.00	1,300.00	3,000.00
1866	7	200.00	950.00	3,150.00
1867	5	200.00	1,100.00	2,900.00
1868	11	200.00	850.00	3,000.00
1869	6	200.00	900.00	2,900.00
1870	6	200.00	700.00	2,250.00
1870S	3	500.00	3,000.00	—
1871	4	225.00	850.00	2,350.00

	Mintage in Thousands	V. Fine	Unc.	Proof
1872	4	225.00	1,000.00	2,250.00
1873	125	200.00	650.00	1,900.00
1874	199	200.00	650.00	1,750.00
1875	420 Pieces	2,800.00	6,000.00	12,000.00
1876	3	225.00	750.00	2,200.00
1877	4	225.00	800.00	2,900.00
1878	3	200.00	800.00	3,000.00
1879	3	200.00	650.00	1,850.00
1880	2	200.00	650.00	2,250.00
1881	8	200.00	650.00	1,600.00
1882	5	200.00	650.00	1,450.00
1883	11	200.00	650.00	1,300.00
1884	6	200.00	650.00	1,100.00
1885	12	200.00	650.00	1,100.00
1886	6	200.00	650.00	1,100.00
1887	9	200.00	650.00	1,100.00
1888	16	200.00	650.00	1,100.00
1889	31	200.00	650.00	1,100.00

42.
QUARTER EAGLES—
1796–1929

($2.50 GOLD PIECES)
LIBERTY CAP TYPE

1796

1796–1807

	Mintage in Thousands	V. Fine	Unc.	—
1796 No Stars	1	6,000.00	20,000.00	—
1796 Stars	432 Pieces	5,500.00	20,000.00	—
1797	427 Pieces	3,750.00	10,000.00	—
1798	1	3,000.00	11,000.00	—
1802 over 1	3	2,250.00	6,500.00	—
1804	3	2,700.00	6,500.00	—
1805	2	2,600.00	6,000.00	—
1806 over 4	2	3,000.00	7,500.00	—
1806 over 5	2	3,250.00	9,000.00	—
1807	7	2,100.00	5,500.00	—

TURBAN HEAD TYPE

1808

1821–1834

1808	3	6,000.00	18,000.00	—
1821	6	2,000.00	7,500.00	—
1824 over 21	3	2,100.00	7,700.00	—
1825	4	2,100.00	7,500.00	—
1826 over 25	1	3,250.00	12,000.00	—
1827	3	2,000.00	7,500.00	—

	Mintage in Thousands	V. Fine	Unc.	—
1829	3	1,600.00	6,250.00	—
1830	5	1,500.00	5,200.00	—
1831	5	1,500.00	5,500.00	—
1832	4	1,500.00	5,500.00	—
1833	4	1,500.00	5,750.00	—
1834 With Motto	4	4,000.00	8,750.00	—

CLASSIC HEAD TYPE

	Mintage in Thousands	Fine	Ex. Fine	Unc.	—
1834 No Motto	112	250.00	425.00	3,750.00	—
1835	131	250.00	425.00	3,750.00	—
1836	548	250.00	425.00	3,750.00	—
1837	45	250.00	425.00	3,750.00	—
1838	47	250.00	425.00	3,750.00	—
1838C	8	500.00	950.00	5,000.00	—
1839	27	250.00	650.00	3,750.00	—
1839C	18	400.00	850.00	4,500.00	—
1839D	14	400.00	900.00	4,850.00	—
1839O	18	350.00	750.00	3,900.00	—

CORONET TYPE

	Mintage in Thousands	Ex. Fine	Unc.	—
1840	19	200.00	650.00	—
1840C	13	350.00	1,000.00	—
1840D	4	700.00	1,300.00	—
1840O	34	250.00	800.00	—
1841 Ex. Rare	—	12,000.00	25,000.00	Proof
1841C	10	450.00	1,500.00	—
1841D	4	600.00	1,500.00	—
1842	3	400.00	1,600.00	—
1842C	7	400.00	1,500.00	—
1842D	5	550.00	1,800.00	—
1842O	20	250.00	900.00	—
1843	101	200.00	500.00	—
1843C	26	300.00	950.00	—
1843D	36	325.00	950.00	—
1843O	364	200.00	500.00	—
1844	7	400.00	950.00	—
1844C	12	350.00	1,300.00	—
1844D	17	300.00	1,100.00	—
1845	91	200.00	500.00	—

	Mintage in Thousands	V. Fine	Unc.	Proof
1845D	19	250.00	1,150.00	—
1845O	4	450.00	2,000.00	—
1846	22	250.00	500.00	—
1846C	5	350.00	1,500.00	—
1846D	19	250.00	1,200.00	—
1846O	66	250.00	500.00	—
1847	30	200.00	500.00	—
1847C	23	200.00	1,250.00	—
1847D	16	200.00	1,250.00	—
1847O	124	200.00	500.00	—
1848	7	500.00	1,350.00	—
1848 CAL above Eagle	1	5,000.00	14,000.00	—
1848C	17	200.00	1,450.00	—
1848D	14	200.00	1,350.00	—
1849	23	200.00	500.00	—
1849C	10	200.00	1,350.00	—
1849D	11	200.00	1,300.00	—
1850	253	200.00	500.00	—
1850C	9	200.00	1,300.00	—
1850D	12	200.00	1,150.00	—
1850O	84	200.00	500.00	—
1851	1373	200.00	500.00	—
1851C	15	225.00	1,500.00	—
1851D	11	200.00	1,500.00	—
1851O	148	200.00	500.00	—
1852	1160	200.00	500.00	—
1852C	8	200.00	1,600.00	—
1852D	4	300.00	1,600.00	—
1852O	140	200.00	500.00	—
1853	1405	200.00	500.00	—
1853D	3	500.00	2,500.00	—
1854	596	200.00	500.00	—
1854C	7	200.00	1,100.00	—
1854D	2	1,650.00	6,000.00	—
1854O	153	200.00	500.00	—
1854S (Rare)	246 Pieces	—	—	—
1855	235	200.00	500.00	12,750.00
1855C	4	600.00	2,500.00	—
1855D	1	1,300.00	6,500.00	—
1856	384	200.00	500.00	8,500.00
1856C	10	200.00	1,500.00	—
1856D	1	2,500.00	500.00	—
1856O	21	200.00	500.00	—
1856S	71	200.00	500.00	—
1857	214	200.00	800.00	5,000.00
1857D	2	550.00	500.00	—
1857O	34	200.00	500.00	—
1857S	69	200.00	600.00	—
1858	47	200.00	500.00	5,500.00
1858C	9	200.00	1,200.00	—
1859	39	200.00	500.00	3,800.00
1859D	2	400.00	2,000.00	—
1859S	15	200.00	800.00	—
1860	23	200.00	500.00	3,000.00
1860C	7	275.00	1,300.00	—
1860S	36	200.00	700.00	—
1861	1248	200.00	500.00	3,000.00

	Mintage in Thousands	Ex. Fine	Unc.	Proof
1861S	24	200.00	800.00	—
1862	99	200.00	500.00	3,000.00
1862S	8	200.00	1,000.00	—
1863	30 Pieces	—	—	21,500.00
1863S	11	200.00	600.00	—
1864	3	750.00	1,200.00	4,000.00
1865	2	950.00	1,800.00	4,000.00
1865S	23	200.00	700.00	—
1866	3	400.00	800.00	3,000.00
1866S	39	200.00	600.00	—
1867	3	450.00	900.00	3,000.00
1867S	28	200.00	650.00	—
1868	4	400.00	800.00	3,000.00
1868S	34	200.00	500.00	—
1869	4	250.00	500.00	3,000.00
1869S	30	200.00	500.00	—
1870	5	300.00	500.00	3,000.00
1870S	16	200.00	500.00	—
1871	5	300.00	500.00	3,000.00
1871S	22	200.00	500.00	—
1872	3	425.00	700.00	3,000.00
1872S	18	200.00	500.00	—
1873	178	200.00	500.00	3,000.00
1873S	27	200.00	500.00	—
1874	4	350.00	600.00	4,000.00
1875	420 Pieces	3,000.00	7,000.00	19,000.00
1875S	12	200.00	500.00	—
1876	4	300.00	850.00	3,000.00
1876S	5	200.00	500.00	—
1877	2	600.00	1,100.00	4,000.00
1877S	35	200.00	500.00	—
1878	286	200.00	500.00	3,800.00
1878S	178	200.00	500.00	—
1879	89	200.00	500.00	3,000.00
1879S	44	200.00	500.00	—
1880	3	250.00	650.00	3,000.00
1881	1	1,100.00	2,250.00	4,500.00
1882	4	250.00	600.00	2,900.00
1883	2	275.00	700.00	2,900.00
1884	2	300.00	600.00	2,900.00
1885	1	950.00	2,000.00	4,300.00
1886	4	250.00	600.00	2,150.00
1887	6	200.00	500.00	2,150.00
1888	16	200.00	500.00	2,150.00
1889	18	200.00	500.00	2,150.00
1890	9	200.00	500.00	2,150.00
1891	11	200.00	500.00	2,150.00
1892	3	200.00	600.00	2,150.00
1893	30	200.00	500.00	2,150.00
1894	4	225.00	500.00	2,150.00
1895	6	200.00	500.00	2,150.00
1896	19	200.00	500.00	2,150.00
1897	30	200.00	500.00	2,150.00
1898	24	200.00	500.00	2,150.00
1899	27	200.00	500.00	2,150.00
1900	67	200.00	500.00	2,150.00
1901	91	200.00	500.00	2,150.00
1902	134	200.00	500.00	2,150.00

	Mintage in Thousands	Ex. Fine	Unc.	Proof
1903	201	200.00	400.00	2,150.00
1904	161	200.00	400.00	2,150.00
1905	218	200.00	400.00	2,150.00
1906	176	200.00	400.00	2,150.00
1907	336	200.00	400.00	2,150.00

INDIAN HEAD TYPE

	Mintage	Ex. Fine	Unc.	Proof
1908	565	150.00	350.00	1,900.00
1909	442	150.00	350.00	1,900.00
1910	493	150.00	350.00	1,900.00
1911	704	150.00	350.00	1,900.00
1911D	56	2,000.00	6,000.00	—
1912	616	150.00	350.00	1,900.00
1913	722	150.00	350.00	1,900.00
1914	240	150.00	300.00	1,900.00
1914D	448	150.00	350.00	—
1915	606	150.00	350.00	1,900.00
1925D	578	150.00	350.00	—
1926	446	150.00	350.00	—
1927	388	150.00	350.00	—
1928	416	150.00	350.00	—
1929	532	150.00	350.00	—

43.
THREE-DOLLAR GOLD PIECES—
1854–1889

	Mintage in Thousands	V. Fine	Unc.	Proof
1854	139	650.00	2,800.00	—
1854D	1	2,500.00	9,000.00	—
1854O	24	650.00	2,800.00	—
1855	51	650.00	2,800.00	—
1855S	7	650.00	3,500.00	—
1856	26	650.00	2,800.00	—
1856S	35	650.00	2,800.00	—
1857	21	650.00	2,800.00	—
1857S	14	650.00	2,800.00	—
1858	2	1,100.00	3,500.00	6,500.00
1859	16	950.00	2,800.00	6,000.00
1860	7	950.00	3,500.00	4,800.00
1860S	7	950.00	2,800.00	
1861	6	950.00	2,800.00	4,900.00
1862	6	950.00	2,800.00	6,100.00
1863	5	950.00	3,500.00	6,100.00
1864	3	950.00	3,500.00	6,300.00
1865	1	950.00	3,500.00	8,250.00
1866	4	950.00	3,500.00	6,500.00
1867	3	950.00	3,500.00	6,000.00
1868	5	950.00	3,500.00	6,000.00
1869	3	950.00	3,500.00	6,000.00
1870	4	950.00	3,500.00	6,000.00
1870S *Very rare*	2 Pieces	—	—	—
1871	1	950.00	3,500.00	6,250.00
1872	2	950.00	3,500.00	6,250.00
1873	About 80 Pieces	—	—	11,500.00
1874	42	650.00	2,800.00	6500.00
1875	20 Pieces	—	—	
1876	45 Pieces	—	—	20,000.00
1877	1	800.00	3,800.00	9,500.00

	Mintage in Thousands	V. Fine	Unc.	Proof
1878	82	650.00	2,800.00	6,000.00
1879	3	1,000.00	3,800.00	5,250.00
1880	1	1,000.00	3,800.00	5,500.00
1881	1	1,100.00	3,800.00	6,800.00
1882	2	1,000.00	3,800.00	5,500.00
1883	1	1,000.00	3,800.00	5,500.00
1884	1	1,000.00	3,800.00	5,000.00
1885	1	1,000.00	3,800.00	5,250.00
1886	1	1,000.00	3,800.00	4,900.00
1887	6	1,000.00	3,800.00	4,100.00
1888	5	1,000.00	3,800.00	4,100.00
1889	2	1,000.00	3,800.00	4,300.00

44.
"STELLA" OR FOUR-DOLLAR GOLD PIECES

	Mintage in Thousands	Proof
1879 Flowing hair	415 Pieces	18,500.00
1879 Coiled hair (Very rare)	10 Pieces	65,000.00
1880 Flowing hair (Very rare).....................................	15 Pieces	38,000.00
1880 Coiled hair (Very rare)	10 Pieces	65,000.00

45.
HALF EAGLES—
1795–1929

($5 GOLD PIECES)
CAPPED BUST TYPE

1795–1798   1795–1807

	Mintage in Thousands	V. Fine	Unc.	—
1795 Small eagle, All Kinds...............	9	3,000.00	8,000.00	—
1795 Large eagle, All Kinds	9	5,000.00	14,000.00	—
1796 over 95	6	3,500.00	9,000.00	—
1797 15 Stars, Small Eagle, All Kinds..	4	4,000.00	12,000.00	—
1797 16 Stars, Small Eagle, All Kinds..	4	4,000.00	12,000.00	—
1798 Small eagle (Very rare).............	—	—	—	—
1797 over 95, Large Eagle.................	(included above)	3,500.00	9,000.00	—
1798 Large eagle, 13 star reverse, All Kinds................................	25	1,200.00	3,000.00	—
1798 Large eagle, 14 star reverse, All Kinds................................	25	2,000.00	5,500.00	—
1799...	7	1,400.00	4,500.00	—
1800...	38	1,400.00	4,500.00	—
1802 over 1....................................	53	1,400.00	4,500.00	—
1803 over 2....................................	34	1,400.00	4,500.00	—
1804...	30	1,400.00	4,500.00	—
1805...	33	1,400.00	4,500.00	—
1806...	64	1,400.00	4,500.00	—
1807...	32	1,400.00	4,500.00	—

LIBERTY CAP TYPE

1807–1812   1813–1834

	Mintage in Thousands	V. Fine	Unc.	
1807..	52	1,150.00	3,500.00	—
1808 over 7, All Kinds	56	1,150.00	3,500.00	—
1808, All Kinds	56	1,150.00	3,500.00	—
1809 over 8.................................	34	1,150.00	3,500.00	—
1810..	100	1,150.00	3,500.00	—
1811..	100	1,150.00	3,500.00	—
1812..	58	1,150.00	3,500.00	—
1813..	95	1,150.00	3,500.00	—
1814 Over 3	15	1,350.00	3,500.00	—
1815 (Rare).................................	1	—	—	—
1818..	49	1,150.00	3,250.00	—
1819..	52	15,000.00	Rare	—
1820..	264	1,300.00	4,000.00	—
1821..	35	4,000.00	9,000.00	—
1822 (Very rare)	18	—	—	—
1823..	14	2,000.00	7,000.00	—
1824..	17	6,000.00	15,000.00	—
1825 over 21, All Kinds	29	3,500.00	8,000.00	—
1825 over 24 (Rare), All Kinds	29	—	—	—
1826..	18	3,500.00	7,000.00	—
1827..	25	7,000.00	Rare	—
1828 over 27, All Kinds	28	4,000.00	9,000.00	—
1828, All Kinds	28	6,000.00	Rare	—
1829 (Rare).................................	57	—	—	—
1830..	126	1,600.00	5,000.00	—
1831..	141	1,600.00	5,000.00	—
1832..	157	4,000.00	10,000.00	—
1833..	194	2,000.00	5,500.00	—
1834..	50	2,500.00	8,500.00	—

CLASSIC HEAD TYPE

	Mintage in Thousands	Ex. Fine	Unc.	—
1834	658	400.00	3.500.00	—
1835	372	400.00	3,500.00	—
1836	553	400.00	3,500.00	—
1837	207	400.00	3,500.00	—
1838	287	400.00	3,500.00	—
1838C	17	1,000.00	5,000.00	—
1838D	21	1,000.00	5,000.00	—

CORONET TYPE

1839–1865

1865–1908

	Mintage in Thousands	Fine	Ex. Fine	Unc.	—
1839	118	150.00	250.00	1,500.00	—
1839C	17	250.00	700.00	1,500.00	—
1839D	19	250.00	700.00	1,500.00	—
1840	137	150.00	200.00	1,500.00	—
1840C	19	200.00	550.00	1,500.00	—
1840D	23	185.00	525.00	1,500.00	—
1840O	40	150.00	285.00	1,500.00	—
1841	16	150.00	300.00	1,500.00	—
1841C	21	225.00	550.00	1,500.00	—
1841D	29	225.00	550.00	1,500.00	—
1841O	50 Pieces	—	—	—	—
1842	28	150.00	250.00	1,500.00	—
1842C	28	200.00	500.00	1,500.00	—
1842D	160	200.00	450.00	1,500.00	—
1842O	16	150.00	350.00	1,500.00	—
1843	611	150.00	200.00	1,200.00	—
1843C	44	200.00	500.00	1,500.00	—
1843D	98	175.00	475.00	1,500.00	—
1843O	101	150.00	300.00	1,500.00	—
1844	340	150.00	200.00	1,200.00	—
1844C	24	235.00	650.00	1,500.00	—
1844D	89	185.00	500.00	1,500.00	—
1844O	365	150.00	225.00	1,250.00	—
1845	417	150.00	200.00	1,200.00	—
1845D	90	175.00	450.00	1,500.00	—
1845O	41	150.00	300.00	1,500.00	—
1846	396	150.00	200.00	1,200.00	—
1846C	13	250.00	700.00	1,500.00	—
1846D	80	165.00	475.00	1,850.00	—
1846O	58	150.00	300.00	1,500.00	—
1847	916	150.00	200.00	1,200.00	—
1847C	84	150.00	450.00	1,500.00	—
1847D	64	150.00	450.00	1,500.00	—
1847O	12	175.00	475.00	1,500.00	—
1848	261	150.00	200.00	1,250.00	—

	Mintage in Thousands	Fine	Ex. Fine	Unc.	Proof
1848C	64	150.00	400.00	1,500.00	—
1848D	47	150.00	400.00	1,500.00	—
1849	133	150.00	200.00	1,200.00	—
1849C	65	150.00	400.00	1,500.00	—
1849D	39	150.00	425.00	1,500.00	—
1850	64	150.00	200.00	1,500.00	—
1850C	64	150.00	425.00	1,500.00	—
1850D	44	150.00	425.00	1,500.00	—
1851	378	150.00	200.00	1,200.00	—
1851C	49	150.00	475.00	1,500.00	—
1851D	63	150.00	450.00	1,500.00	—
1851O	41	150.00	350.00	1,500.00	—
1852	574	150.00	200.00	1,200.00	—
1852C	73	150.00	400.00	1,500.00	—
1852D	92	150.00	400.00	1,500.00	—
1853	306	150.00	200.00	1,200.00	—
1853C	66	150.00	400.00	1,500.00	—
1853D	90	150.00	400.00	1,500.00	—
1854	161	150.00	200.00	1,200.00	—
1854C	39	160.00	425.00	1,500.00	—
1854D	56	150.00	400.00	1,500.00	—
1854O	46	150.00	350.00	1,500.00	—
1854S (Rare)	268 Pieces	—	—	35,000.00	—
1855	117	150.00	200.00	1,200.00	7,000.00
1855C	40	150.00	400.00	1,500.00	—
1855D	22	150.00	400.00	1,500.00	—
1855O	11	150.00	400.00	1,500.00	—
1855S	61	150.00	200.00	1,500.00	—
1856	198	150.00	200.00	1,200.00	7,000.00
1856C	28	150.00	400.00	1,500.00	—
1856D	20	150.00	400.00	1,500.00	—
1856O	10	160.00	500.00	1,500.00	—
1856S	105	150.00	200.00	1,500.00	—
1857	98	150.00	200.00	1,200.00	6,500.00
1857C	31	150.00	400.00	1,500.00	—
1857D	17	150.00	400.00	1,500.00	—
1857O	13	160.00	500.00	1,500.00	—
1857S	87	150.00	200.00	1,500.00	—
1858	15	150.00	300.00	1,500.00	6,750.00
1858C	39	150.00	400.00	1,500.00	—
1858D	15	150.00	400.00	1,500.00	—
1858S	19	150.00	300.00	1,500.00	—
1859	17	150.00	300.00	1,500.00	4,000.00
1859C	32	150.00	375.00	1,500.00	—
1859D	10	190.00	700.00	1,500.00	—
1859S	13	150.00	350.00	1,500.00	—
1860	20	150.00	240.00	1,500.00	3,250.00
1860C	15	175.00	550.00	1,500.00	—
1860D	15	175.00	600.00	1,500.00	—
1860S	21	150.00	250.00	1,500.00	—
1861	688	150.00	200.00	1,200.00	3,000.00
1861C	7	750.00	1,600.00	3,500.00	—
1861D	2	1,900.00	5,000.00	8,500.00	—
1861S	18	150.00	250.00	1,500.00	—
1862	4	200.00	450.00	1,500.00	3,000.00
1862S	10	160.00	450.00	1,500.00	—
1863	2	300.00	600.00	1,900.00	4,500.00
1863S	17	150.00	400.00	1,500.00	—

	Mintage in Thousands	Fine	Ex. Fine	Unc.	Proof
1864..................................	4	235.00	600.00	1,700.00	6,500.00
1864S.................................	4	450.00	1,650.00	4,500.00	—
1865..................................	1	350.00	650.00	1,500.00	5,500.00
1865S.................................	28	155.00	225.00	1,200.00	—
1866 S No Motto	9	155.00	450.00	1,300.00	—
1866 Motto on Reverse	7	200.00	550.00	900.00	3,750.00
1866S.................................	35	155.00	400.00	900.00	—
1867..................................	7	155.00	375.00	800.00	5,000.00
1867S.................................	29	155.00	225.00	600.00	—
1868..................................	6	155.00	350.00	550.00	4,000.00
1868S.................................	52	155.00	250.00	600.00	—
1869..................................	2	250.00	650.00	1,000.00	4,000.00
1869S.................................	31	155.00	275.00	550.00	—
1870..................................	4	160.00	450.00	750.00	4,000.00
1870CC	7	800.00	1,900.00	—	—
1870S.................................	17	155.00	275.00	600.00	—
1871..................................	3	200.00	475.00	700.00	4,500.00
1871CC	21	225.00	650.00	1,400.00	—
1871S.................................	25	155.00	250.00	600.00	—
1872..................................	2	350.00	650.00	1,000.00	4,500.00
1872CC	17	250.00	750.00	1,150.00	—
1872S.................................	36	155.00	225.00	400.00	—
1873..................................	112	155.00	165.00	225.00	4,500.00
1873CC	7	275.00	800.00	1,300.00	—
1873S.................................	31	155.00	175.00	450.00	—
1874..................................	4	200.00	550.00	1,100.00	5,500.00
1874CC	21	155.00	450.00	1,100.00	—
1874S.................................	16	155.00	275.00	450.00	—
1875..................................	220 Pieces	Rare	Rare	Rare	Rare
1875CC	12	275.00	800.00	1,200.00	—
1875S.................................	9	155.00	450.00	750.00	—
1876..................................	1	350.00	850.00	1,850.00	6,000.00
1876CC	7	225.00	700.00	1,200.00	—
1876S.................................	4	225.00	800.00	1,500.00	—
1877..................................	1	350.00	850.00	1,600.00	6,500.00
1877CC	9	225.00	600.00	1,200.00	—
1877S.................................	27	155.00	165.00	300.00	—
1878..................................	132	155.00	165.00	225.00	3,250.00
1878CC	9	550.00	1,800.00	—	—
1878S.................................	145	155.00	165.00	225.00	—
1879..................................	302	155.00	165.00	225.00	2,250.00
1879CC	17	155.00	300.00	600.00	—
1879S.................................	426	155.00	165.00	225.00	—
1880..................................	3166	155.00	165.00	225.00	2,250.00
1880CC	51	155.00	165.00	300.00	—
1880S.................................	1349	155.00	165.00	225.00	—
1881..................................	5709	155.00	165.00	225.00	2,250.00
1881CC	14	155.00	250.00	500.00	—
1881S.................................	969	155.00	165.00	225.00	—
1882..................................	2515	155.00	165.00	225.00	2,250.00
1882CC	83	155.00	190.00	300.00	—
1882S.................................	970	155.00	165.00	225.00	—
1883..................................	233	155.00	165.00	225.00	2,250.00
1883CC	13	155.00	250.00	400.00	—
1883S.................................	83	155.00	165.00	225.00	—
1884..................................	191	155.00	165.00	225.00	2,250.00
1884CC	16	155.00	250.00	400.00	—
1884S.................................	177	155.00	165.00	225.00	—

	Mintage in Thousands	Fine	Ex. Fine	Unc.	Proof
1885	602	155.00	165.00	210.00	2,250.00
1885S	1212	155.00	165.00	210.00	—
1886	388	155.00	165.00	210.00	2,250.00
1886S	3268	155.00	165.00	210.00	—
1887	87 Pieces	—	—	—	15,000.00
1887S	1912	155.00	165.00	210.00	—
1888	18	155.00	165.00	210.00	2,500.00
1888S	294	155.00	165.00	210.00	—
1889	8	200.00	350.00	700.00	2,500.00
1890	4	250.00	450.00	800.00	2,500.00
1890CC	54	155.00	185.00	300.00	—
1891	61	155.00	165.00	210.00	1,450.00
1891CC	208	155.00	175.00	300.00	—
1892	754	155.00	165.00	210.00	1,450.00
1892CC	83	155.00	175.00	300.00	—
1892O	10	400.00	900.00	1,500.00	—
1892S	298	155.00	165.00	210.00	—
1893	1528	155.00	165.00	210.00	1,450.00
1893CC	60	155.00	165.00	275.00	—
1893O	110	155.00	225.00	400.00	—
1893S	224	155.00	165.00	210.00	—
1894	958	155.00	165.00	210.00	1,450.00
1894O	17	155.00	225.00	475.00	—
1894S	56	155.00	165.00	210.00	—
1895	1346	155.00	165.00	210.00	1,450.00
1895S	112	155.00	165.00	210.00	—
1896	59	155.00	165.00	210.00	1,450.00
1896S	155	155.00	165.00	210.00	—
1897	868	155.00	165.00	210.00	1,450.00
1897S	354	155.00	165.00	210.00	—
1898	633	155.00	165.00	210.00	1,450.00
1898S	1397	155.00	165.00	210.00	—
1899	1,711	155.00	165.00	210.00	1,450.00
1899S	1545	155.00	165.00	210.00	—
1900	1406	155.00	165.00	210.00	1,450.00
1900S	329	155.00	165.00	210.00	—
1901	616	155.00	165.00	210.00	1,450.00
1901S	3648	155.00	165.00	210.00	—
1902	173	155.00	165.00	210.00	1,450.00
1902S	939	155.00	165.00	210.00	—
1903	227	155.00	165.00	210.00	1,450.00
1903S	1855	155.00	165.00	210.00	—
1904	392	155.00	165.00	210.00	1,450.00
1904S	97	155.00	165.00	225.00	—
1905	302	155.00	165.00	210.00	1,450.00
1905S	881	155.00	165.00	210.00	—
1906	349	155.00	165.00	210.00	1,450.00
1906D	320	155.00	165.00	210.00	—
1906S	598	155.00	165.00	210.00	—
1907	626	155.00	165.00	210.00	1,140.00
1907D	888	155.00	165.00	210.00	—
1908	422	155.00	165.00	210.00	1,450.00

INDIAN HEAD TYPE

	Mintage in Thousands	Ex. Fine	Unc.	Proof
1908	578	180.00	600.00	3,000.00
1908D	148	180.00	600.00	—
1908S	82	650.00	4,000.00	—
1909	627	180.00	600.00	3,000.00
1909D	3424	180.00	600.00	—
1909O	34	1,500.00	9,000.00	—
1909S	297	180.00	2,500.00	—
1910	604	180.00	600.00	3,000.00
1910D	194	180.00	1,500.00	—
1910S	770	200.00	2,500.00	—
1911	915	180.00	600.00	3,000.00
1911D	73	600.00	6,000.00	—
1911S	1416	180.00	1,500.00	—
1912	790	180.00	600.00	3,000.00
1912S	392	180.00	2,400.00	—
1913	916	180.00	600.00	3,000.00
1913S	408	450.00	5,500.00	—
1914	247	180.00	600.00	3,000.00
1914D	247	180.00	800.00	—
1914S	263	180.00	1,900.00	—
1915	588	180.00	600.00	3,500.00
1915S	164	190.00	3,500.00	—
1916S	240	180.00	1,700.00	—
1929	662	4,500.00	9,500.00	—

46.
EAGLES—
1795–1933

($10 GOLD PIECES)

BUST TYPE

1795–1797 1797–1804

	Mintage in Thousands	V. Fine	Unc.	—
1795	6	3,500.00	18,500.00	—
1796	4	3,500.00	17,500.00	—
1797 Small Eagle	4	3,500.00	21,000.00	—
1797 Large Eagle	11	2,500.00	10,000.00	—
1798 over 97, 9 Stars Left, 4 Right	1	4,000.00	15,000.00	—
1798 over 97, 7 Stars Left, 6 Right	1	7,500.00	33,000.00	—
1799	37	2,000.00	10,000.00	—
1800	6	2,000.00	11,000.00	—
1801	44	2,000.00	10,000.00	—
1803	15	2,000.00	10,000.00	—
1804	4	3,500.00	11,000.00	—

170

	Mintage *in Thousands*	Ex. Fine	Unc.	—
1838	7	1,400.00	5,000.00	—
1839	38	1,100.00	4,500.00	—

1840–1865   **1866–1907**

1840	47	375.00	3,500.00	—
1841	63	375.00	3,500.00	—
1841O	3	950.00	3,500.00	—
1842	82	375.00	3,500.00	—
1842O	27	375.00	3,500.00	—
1843	75	375.00	3,500.00	—
1843O	175	375.00	3,500.00	—
1844	6	800.00	3,500.00	—
1844O	119	375.00	3,500.00	—
1845	26	375.00	3,500.00	—
1845O	48	375.00	3,500.00	—
1846	20	375.00	3,500.00	—
1846O	82	375.00	3,500.00	—
1847	862	375.00	3,500.00	—
1847O	572	375.00	3,500.00	—
1848	145	375.00	3,500.00	—
1848O	36	375.00	3,500.00	—
1849	654	375.00	3,500.00	—
1849O	24	375.00	3,500.00	—
1850	291	375.00	3,500.00	—
1850O	58	375.00	3,500.00	—
1851	176	375.00	3,500.00	—
1851O	263	375.00	3,500.00	—
1852	263	375.00	3,500.00	—

	Mintage in Thousands	Ex. Fine	Unc.	Proof
1852O	18	375.00	3,500.00	—
1853	201	375.00	3,500.00	—
1853O	51	375.00	3,500.00	—
1854	54	375.00	3,500.00	—
1854O	53	375.00	3,500.00	—
1854S	124	375.00	3,500.00	—
1855	122	375.00	3,500.00	8,000.00
1855O	18	375.00	3,500.00	—
1855S	9	800.00	3,500.00	—
1856	60	375.00	3,500.00	6,000.00
1856O	15	375.00	3,500.00	—
1856S	68	375.00	3,500.00	—
1857	17	375.00	3,500.00	6,000.00
1857O	6	850.00	3,500.00	—
1857S	26	375.00	3,500.00	—
1858	3	5,500.00	—	—
1858O	20	375.00	3,500.00	—
1858S	12	375.00	3,500.00	—
1859	16	375.00	3,500.00	6,000.00
1859O	2	1,500.00	3,500.00	—
1859S	7	850.00	3,500.00	—
1860	15	375.00	3,500.00	6,000.00
1860O	11	375.00	3,500.00	—
1860S	5	750.00	3,500.00	—
1861	113	375.00	3,500.00	6,000.00
1861S	16	375.00	3,500.00	—
1862	11	375.00	3,500.00	6,250.00
1862S	13	375.00	3,500.00	—
1863	1	2,850.00	4,500.00	9,500.00
1863S	10	550.00	3,500.00	—
1864	4	750.00	3,500.00	8,500.00
1864S	3	2,500.00	—	—
1865	4	1,150.00	3,500.00	7,500.00
1865S	17	850.00	3,500.00	—
1866S No Motto	9	1,400.00	3,500.00	—
1866 With Motto	4	600.00	3,500.00	7,000.00
1866S	12	375.00	900.00	—
1867	3	700.00	1,400.00	7,250.00
1867S	9	400.00	900.00	—
1868	11	300.00	750.00	7,000.00
1868S	14	300.00	700.00	—
1869	2	900.00	1,800.00	7,500.00
1869S	6	500.00	1,150.00	—
1870	4	600.00	1,200.00	7,000.00
1870CC	6	1,350.00	—	—
1870S	8	500.00	950.00	—
1871	2	1,250.00	2,900.00	7,500.00
1871CC	7	1,150.00	—	—
1871S	17	300.00	750.00	—
1872	2	1,250.00	2,500.00	7,250.00
1872CC	6	1,100.00	2,000.00	—
1872S	17	300.00	750.00	—
1873	1	3,000.00	5,500.00	9,500.00
1873CC	5	2,250.00	3,750.00	—
1873S	12	300.00	700.00	—
1874	53	300.00	400.00	7,500.00
1874CC	17	500.00	1,000.00	—

	Mintage in Thousands	Ex. Fine	Unc.	Proof
1874S	10	350.00	700.00	—
1875 (Very rare)	120 Pieces	—	—	—
1875CC	8	1,000.00	1,500.00	—
1876	1	3,000.00	4,500.00	8,000.00
1876CC	5	1,100.00	2,250.00	—
1876S	5	750.00	1,250.00	—
1877	1	2,500.00	4,500.00	15,000.00
1877CC	3	1,100.00	2,200.00	—
1877S	17	300.00	375.00	—
1878	74	300.00	375.00	7,000.00
1878CC	3	1,400.00	2,600.00	—
1878S	26	300.00	375.00	—
1879	385	300.00	375.00	5,500.00
1879CC	2	4,250.00	7,000.00	—
1879O	2	1,750.00	3,750.00	—
1879S	224	300.00	375.00	—
1880	1645	300.00	375.00	5,000.00
1880CC	11	300.00	400.00	—
1880O	9	300.00	500.00	—
1880S	506	300.00	375.00	—
1881	3877	300.00	375.00	5,000.00
1881CC	24	300.00	425.00	—
1881O	8	300.00	600.00	—
1881S	970	300.00	375.00	—
1882	2324	300.00	375.00	5,000.00
1882CC	17	375.00	600.00	—
1882O	11	300.00	375.00	—
1882S	132	300.00	375.00	—
1883	209	300.00	375.00	5,000.00
1883CC	12	300.00	375.00	—
1883O	1	3,500.00	6,000.00	—
1883S	38	300.00	375.00	—
1884	77	300.00	375.00	8,500.00
1884CC	10	300.00	400.00	—
1884S	124	300.00	375.00	—
1885	254	300.00	375.00	4,000.00
1885S	228	300.00	375.00	—
1886	236	300.00	375.00	4,000.00
1886S	826	300.00	375.00	—
1887	54	300.00	375.00	4,000.00
1887S	817	300.00	375.00	—
1888	133	300.00	375.00	4,000.00
1888O	21	300.00	375.00	—
1888S	649	300.00	375.00	—
1889	4	475.00	850.00	4,750.00
1889S	425	300.00	375.00	—
1890	58	300.00	375.00	4,000.00
1890CC	18	300.00	400.00	—
1891	92	300.00	375.00	4,500.00
1891CC	104	300.00	375.00	—
1892	798	300.00	375.00	4,000.00
1892CC	40	300.00	375.00	—
1892O	29	300.00	375.00	—
1892S	116	300.00	375.00	—
1893	1841	300.00	375.00	4,000.00
1893CC	14	300.00	375.00	—
1893O	17	300.00	375.00	—

	Mintage in Thousands	Ex. Fine	Unc.	Proof
1893S	141	300.00	400.00	—
1894	2471	300.00	400.00	4,000.00
1894O	108	300.00	400.00	—
1894S	25	300.00	400.00	—
1895	568	300.00	400.00	4,000.00
1895O	98	300.00	400.00	—
1895S	49	300.00	400.00	—
1896	76	300.00	400.00	4,000.00
1896S	124	300.00	400.00	—
1897	1000	300.00	400.00	4,000.00
1897O	43	300.00	400.00	—
1897S	235	300.00	400.00	—
1898	812	300.00	400.00	3,750.00
1898S	474	300.00	400.00	—
1899	1262	300.00	400.00	3,750.00
1899O	37	300.00	400.00	—
1899S	841	300.00	400.00	—
1900	294	300.00	400.00	3,500.00
1900S	81	300.00	400.00	—
1901	1719	300.00	400.00	3,500.00
1901O	72	300.00	400.00	—
1901S	2813	300.00	400.00	—
1902	83	300.00	400.00	3,500.00
1902S	470	300.00	400.00	—
1903	126	300.00	400.00	3,500.00
1903O	113	300.00	400.00	—
1903S	538	300.00	400.00	—
1904	162	300.00	400.00	3,500.00
1904O	109	300.00	400.00	—
1905	201	300.00	400.00	3,500.00
1905S	369	300.00	400.00	—
1906	165	300.00	400.00	3,500.00
1906D	981	300.00	400.00	—
1906O	87	300.00	400.00	—
1906S	457	300.00	400.00	—
1907 All Kinds	1204	300.00	100.00	3,500.00
1907D	1030	300.00	400.00	—
1907S	211	300.00	400.00	—

INDIAN HEAD TYPE

No Motto   Motto

	Mintage in Thousands	Ex. Fine	Unc.	Proof
1907 Wire Edge, Periods before and after Legends	500 Pieces	10,000.00	15,000.00	10,000.00
1907 Rolled Edge, Periods (Rare)	42 Pieces	—	—	—
1907 No Periods	239	450.00	900.00	—
1908 No Motto	34	600.00	2,400.00	—
1908D No Motto	210	450.00	2,500.00	—
1908 With Motto	341	450.00	1,100.00	4,000.00
1908D	837	450.00	1,200.00	—
1908S	60	650.00	4,500.00	—
1909	185	450.00	800.00	4,000.00
1909D	122	450.00	900.00	—
1909S	292	450.00	2,500.00	—
1910	319	450.00	800.00	4,000.00
1910D	2357	450.00	800.00	—
1910S	811	450.00	2,100.00	—
1911	506	450.00	700.00	4,000.00
1911D	30	1,100.00	8,000.00	—
1911S	51	600.00	4,000.00	—
1912	405	450.00	700.00	4,000.00
1912S	300	450.00	3,000.00	—
1913	442	450.00	750.00	4,000.00
1913S	66	1,100.00	15,000.00	—
1914	151	450.00	800.00	4,500.00
1914D	344	450.00	850.00	—
1914S	208	450.00	2,500.00	—
1915	351	450.00	750.00	4,000.00
1915S	59	700.00	4,000.00	—
1916S	139	450.00	2,000.00	—
1920S (Rare)	127	20,000.00	40,000.00	—
1926	1014	450.00	700.00	—
1930S	96	3,000.00	14,000.00	—
1932	4463	450.00	700.00	—
1933 (Rare)	313	—	45,000.00	—

47.
DOUBLE EAGLES—
1850–1932

($20 GOLD PIECES)

CORONET TYPE

1849–1865   1866–1907

	Mintage in Thousands	Ex. Fine	Unc.
1849 Unique—U.S. Mint Collection			
1850	1170	700.00	2,200.00
1850O	141	700.00	3,000.00
1851	2087	700.00	2,200.00
1851O	315	700.00	2,500.00
1852	2053	700.00	2,200.00
1852O	190	700.00	2,700.00
1853	1261	700.00	2,200.00
1853O	71	800.00	2,900.00
1854	758	700.00	2,200.00
1854O (Rare)	3	—	—
1854S	141	700.00	2,950.00
1855	365	700.00	2,200.00
1855O	8	1,900.00	3,500.00
1855S	880	700.00	2,200.00
1856	330	700.00	2,200.00
1856O (Rare)	2	—	—
1856S	1190	700.00	2,200.00
1857	439	700.00	2,200.00
1857O	30	950.00	2,800.00
1857S	971	700.00	2,200.00
1858	212	700.00	2,200.00
1858O	35	900.00	3,000.00
1858S	847	700.00	2,200.00
1859	44	700.00	2,200.00

	Mintage in Thousands	Ex. Fine	Unc.
1859O	9	2,250.00	5,000.00
1859S	636	700.00	2,200.00
1860	578	700.00	2,200.00
1860O	7	2,750.00	5,500.00
1860S	545	700.00	2,200.00
1861	2976	700.00	2,200.00
1861O	18	2,000.00	6,500.00
1861S	768	700.00	2,200.00
1862	92	700.00	2,200.00
1862S	854	700.00	2,200.00
1863	143	700.00	2,300.00
1863S	967	700.00	2,200.00
1864	204	700.00	2,200.00
1864S	794	700.00	2,200.00
1865	351	700.00	2,200.00
1865S	1043	700.00	2,200.00
1866S No Motto	—	1,000.00	2,200.00
1866 With Motto	699	700.00	1,100.00
1866S	842	700.00	850.00
1867	251	700.00	800.00
1867S	921	700.00	950.00
1868	99	700.00	950.00
1868S	838	700.00	800.00
1869	175	700.00	900.00
1869S	687	700.00	850.00
1870	155	700.00	850.00
1870CC (Very Rare)	4	—	—
1870S	982	700.00	950.00
1871	80	700.00	900.00
1871CC	15	1,800.00	—
1871S	928	700.00	800.00
1872	252	700.00	800.00
1872CC	30	800.00	1,750.00
1872S	780	700.00	800.00
1873	1710	700.00	800.00
1873CC	22	1,000.00	2,000.00
1873S	1041	700.00	800.00
1874	367	700.00	800.00
1874CC	115	700.00	850.00
1874S	1214	700.00	800.00
1875	296	700.00	800.00
1875CC	111	700.00	800.00
1875S	1230	700.00	800.00
1876	584	700.00	800.00
1876CC	138	700.00	800.00
1876S	1597	700.00	800.00
1877	398	700.00	800.00
1877CC	43	700.00	1,350.00
1877S	1735	700.00	800.00
1878	544	700.00	800.00
1878CC	13	800.00	2,000.00
1878S	1739	700.00	800.00
1879	208	700.00	800.00
1879CC	11	1,000.00	2,200.00
1879O	2	3,800.00	6,500.00
1879S	1224	700.00	800.00
1880	51	700.00	950.00

	Mintage in Thousands	Ex. Fine	Unc.
1880S	836	700.00	800.00
1881	2	4,500.00	7,500.00
1881S	727	700.00	800.00
1882	1	8,000.00	12,000.00
1882CC	39	700.00	900.00
1882S	1125	700.00	800.00
1883 (Rare)	92 Pieces	—	—
1883CC	60	700.00	800.00
1883S	1189	700.00	800.00
1884 (Rare)	71 Pieces	—	—
1884CC	81	700.00	800.00
1884S	916	700.00	800.00
1885	1	5,000.00	8,000.00
1885CC	9	800.00	1,600.00
1885S	684	700.00	800.00
1886	1	7,000.00	11,500.00
1887 (Rare)	121 Pieces	—	—
1887S	283	700.00	800.00
1888	226	700.00	800.00
1888S	860	700.00	800.00
1889	44	700.00	800.00
1889CC	31	700.00	900.00
1889S	775	700.00	800.00
1890	76	700.00	800.00
1890CC	91	700.00	800.00
1890S	803	700.00	800.00
1891	1	2,800.00	5,000.00
1891CC	5	1,600.00	2,600.00
1891S	1288	700.00	800.00
1892	5	1,500.00	2,850.00
1892CC	27	700.00	850.00
1892S	930	700.00	800.00
1893	344	700.00	800.00
1893CC	18	700.00	1,450.00
1893S	996	700.00	800.00
1894	1369	700.00	800.00
1894S	1049	700.00	800.00
1895	1115	700.00	800.00
1895S	1144	700.00	800.00
1896	793	700.00	800.00
1896S	1404	700.00	800.00
1897	1383	700.00	800.00
1897S	1470	700.00	800.00
1898	170	700.00	800.00
1898S	2575	700.00	800.00
1899	1669	700.00	800.00
1899S	2010	700.00	800.00
1900	1875	700.00	800.00
1900S	2460	700.00	800.00
1901	112	700.00	800.00
1901S	1596	700.00	800.00
1902	31	700.00	875.00
1902S	1754	700.00	800.00
1903	287	700.00	800.00
1903S	954	700.00	800.00
1904	6257	700.00	800.00
1904S	5134	700.00	800.00

	Mintage in Thousands	Ex. Fine	Unc.
1905	59	700.00	950.00
1905S	1813	700.00	800.00
1906	70	700.00	900.00
1906D	620	700.00	800.00
1906S	2066	700.00	800.00
1907	1452	700.00	800.00
1907D	842	700.00	800.00
1907S	2166	700.00	800.00

SAINT-GAUDENS TYPE

1907 High Relief Roman Numerals (MCMVII) Wire Rim, All Kinds	11	5,500.00	2,000.00
1907 High Relief Flat Rim, All Kinds	11	5,500.00	2,000.00

1907–1908   1908–1932 Motto

	Mintage	Ex. Fine	Unc.
1907 No Motto	362	700.00	800.00
1908	4272	700.00	800.00
1908D	664	700.00	800.00
1908 With Motto	156	700.00	800.00
1908D	350	700.00	800.00
1908S	22	1,500.00	4,500.00
1909 over 8, All Kinds	161	700.00	1,300.00
1909, All Kinds	161	700.00	1,150.00
1909D	53	1,000.00	2,850.00
1909S	2775	700.00	800.00
1910	482	700.00	800.00
1910D	429	700.00	800.00
1910S	2128	700.00	800.00
1911	197	700.00	800.00
1911D	847	700.00	800.00

	Mintage in Thousands	Ex. Fine	Unc.
1911S	776	700.00	800.00
1912	150	700.00	800.00
1913	169	700.00	800.00
1913D	394	700.00	800.00
1913S	34	800.00	1,350.00
1914	95	700.00	800.00
1914D	453	700.00	800.00
1914S	1498	700.00	800.00
1915	152	700.00	800.00
1915S	568	700.00	800.00
1916S	796	700.00	800.00
1920	228	700.00	800.00
1920S	558	11,000.00	20,000.00
1921	530	20,000.00	35,000.00
1922	1376	700.00	800.00
1922S	2658	700.00	1,100.00
1923	566	700.00	800.00
1923D	1702	700.00	800.00
1924	4324	700.00	800.00
1924D	3050	900.00	2,000.00
1924S	2928	850.00	1,700.00
1925	2832	700.00	800.00
1925D	2939	1,000.00	2,800.00
1925S	3777	950.00	2,900.00
1926	817	700.00	800.00
1926D	481	1,500.00	3,500.00
1926S	2042	900.00	1,650.00
1927	2947	700.00	800.00
1927D (Rare)	180	—	—
1927S	3107	5,500.00	12,500.00
1928	8816	700.00	800.00
1929	1780	4,500.00	10,000.00
1930S	74	11,000.00	20,000.00
1931	2938	10,000.00	15,000.00
1931D	107	10,500.00	18,000.00
1932	1102	12,000.00	25,000.00

(Note: Nearly all dates through 1915 of Double Eagles exist in Proof; all are very rare and perfect pieces are valued upwards of 10,000.00 each.)

48.
PRIVATE AND TERRITORIAL GOLD COINS

GEORGIA

1830 $2.50 TEMPLETON REID (Very rare)
1830 $5.00 TEMPLETON REID (Very rare)
1830 TEN DOLLARS (Very rare)
NO DATE, TEN DOLLARS (Very rare)

NORTH CAROLINA

	Fine	Unc.	—
$1.00 CHRISTOPHER BECHTLER	200.00	1,000.00	—
$2.50	400.00	1,500.00	—
$5.00	1,450.00	1,400.00	—

CALIFORNIA

NORRIS, GRIEF AND NORRIS

1849 $5.00	1,500.00	6,000.00	—

	Fine	Ex. Fine	
1849 $10.00	800.00	3,000.00	—
1849 $5.00	400.00	1,000.00	—
1850 $5.00	500.00	1,100.00	—
1852 $10.00	800.00	2,000.00	—

AUGUSTUS HUMBERT
U.S. ASSAYER

1851 FIFTY DOLLARS 880 THOUS. "Target" Reverse	3,250.00	9,000.00	—
1851 FIFTY DOLLARS 887 THOUS. "Target" Reverse	3,500.00	9,500.00	—
1852 FIFTY DOLLARS 887 THOUS. No "Target"	3,000.00	7,500.00	—
1852 FIFTY DOLLARS 900 THOUS.	3,000.00	8,500.00	—
1851 50 D Several Varieties: AUGUSTUS HUMBERT UNITED STATES ASSAYER OF GOLD CALIFORNIA 1851	3,000.00	9,000.00	—
1852 TWENTY DOLLARS 1852 over 1	2,800.00	6,500.00	—
1853 TWENTY DOLLARS 884 THOUS.	3,000.00	9,000.00	—
1853 TWENTY DOLLARS 900 THOUS.	600.00	1,500.00	—

	Fine	Ex. Fine	
1852 TEN DOLLARS 1852 over 1	800.00	1,500.00	—
1852 TEN DOLLARS 884 THOUS.	450.00	1,000.00	—
1853 TEN DOLLARS 884 THOUS. (Rare)	—	—	—
1853 TEN DOLLARS 900 THOUS.	1,000.00	3,000.00	—

BALDWIN & COMPANY

	Fine	Unc.	
1850 TEN DOLLARS	7,500.00	—	—
1851 TWENTY DOLLARS (Rare)	—	—	—
1851 TEN DOLLARS	4,000.00	12,000.00	—
1850 FIVE DOLLARS	1,750.00	6,000.00	—

SCHULTZ & COMPANY
1851 FIVE DOLLARS	10,000.00	—	—

DUNBAR & COMPANY
1851 FIVE DOLLARS (Rare)	—	—	—

WASS, MOLITOR & COMPANY

	Fine	Ex. Fine	
1855 FIFTY DOLLARS	6,500.00	15,000.00	—
1855 TWENTY DOLLARS, Small Head	3,000.00	8,000.00	—
1855 TWENTY DOLLARS, Large Head (Rare)..	—	—	—
1852 TEN DOLLARS, Small Head	1,400.00	4,000.00	—
1852 TEN DOLLARS, Large Head	750.00	2,000.00	—
1855 TEN DOLLARS	2,000.00	6,000.00	—
1852 FIVE DOLLARS, Small Head	1,200.00	3,000.00	—
1852 FIVE DOLLARS, Large Head ..,.............	1,000.00	2,500.00	—

KELLOGG & COMPANY

1855 FIFTY DOLLARS (Rare)	—	—	—
1854 TWENTY DOLLARS.............................	700.00	1,500.00	—
1855 TWENTY DOLLARS.............................	725.00	1,600.00	—

There were also issued, in California, round and octagonal twenty-five-cent, fifty-cent, and one-dollar gold pieces of which there are many copies and "charms." Genuine pieces must have their denomination upon them, i.e. "½ Dol.," or "½ Dollar," or "half dollar," etc. These coins are valued as follows:

	Fine	Unc.	—
.25 Round Indian or Liberty Heads	40.00	160.00	—
.25 Octagonal Indian or Liberty Heads	40.00	160.00	—
.50 Round Indian or Liberty Heads	50.00	185.00	—
.50 Octagonal Indian or Liberty Heads	50.00	185.00	—
1.00 Round Indian Heads	550.00	1,750.00	—
1.00 Octagonal Indian or Liberty Heads	90.00	600.00	—
1.00 Round Liberty Heads	600.00	1,900.00	—

(Washington Heads bring about 50% more.)

OREGON

OREGON EXCHANGE COMPANY

	Fine	Ex. Fine	V. Fine
1849 TEN DOLLARS (Rare)	—	—	
1849 FIVE DOLLARS	3,500.00	7,000.00	—

UTAH

MORMON GOLD
1849 TWENTY DOLLARS (Rare)	—	—
1849 TEN DOLLARS (Rare)	—	—

	Fine	Ex. Fine	
1849 FIVE DOLLARS	1,000.00	1,850.00	—

1849 TWO AND ONE HALF DOLLARS	1,000.00	2,000.00	—
1850 FIVE DOLLARS	850.00	2,000.00	—

1860 FIVE DOLLARS	2,500.00	5,000.00	—

COLORADO
CLARK, GRUBER & COMPANY

1860 TWENTY DOLLARS (Rare)...................	—	—	—
1860 TEN DOLLARS	1,250.00	3,300.00	—
1861 TWENTY DOLLARS............................	3,000.00	10,000.00	—

1861 TEN DOLLARS	900.00	2,000.00	—
1861 FIVE DOLLARS	800.00	1,600.00	—
1861 TWO AND ONE HALF DOLLARS	500.00	1,000.00	

CLARK & CO.

1860 FIVE DOLLARS	750.00	1,750.00	—
1860 TWO AND ONE HALF DOLLARS	550.00	1,250.00	

JOHN PARSONS & COMPANY

(1861) Undated 2½ D (Rare)	—	—	—
(1861) Undated FIVE D (Rare)	—	—	—

J. J. CONWAY & COMPANY

(1861) 2½ DOLL'S (Rare)	—	—	—
(1861) FIVE DOLLARS (Rare)	—	—	—
1861 TEN DOLLARS (Very rare)	—	—	—

49.
HARD TIMES
TOKENS

These are tokens, usually satirically political in nature, which were privately struck and issued in the period 1832–1844. The tokens are copper or brass and are predominantly the same size at the large one-cent piece of the period. Descriptions of the major types follow. (Tradesman's or advertising tokens of the same approximate period encompass hundreds of varieties which are outside the scope of this listing. The value for the more common of the commercial varieties are: Good $1.50; Fine $3.00; Ex. fine $5.00; Unc. $20.00.)

Type	Good	Fine	Ex.Fine	Unc.
1. Jackson Head right/ Legend in wreath	200.00	300.00	500.00	1,500.00
2. Jackson Bust Right/ Legend	25.00	40.00	65.00	125.00
3. Jackson Bust Facing/ Eagle	35.00	75.00	150.00	250.00
4. Van Buren Bust Facing/ Chest	200.00	300.00	500.00	900.00
5. Van Buren Bust Right/ Eagle	20.00	45.00	100.00	250.00
6. Van Buren Bust Left/ Safe	7.00	15.00	35.00	100.00
7. Seward Bust Left/ Eagle	12.00	25.00	50.00	125.00
8. Verplank Bust Left/ Eagle	10.00	22.00	45.00	100.00
9. Ship Left/Victorious Whigs of New York	50.00	100.00	175.00	350.00
10. Liberty Cap/Ship	150.00	250.00	800.00	—
11. Cow Right/Ship	15.00	35.00	75.00	200.00
12. Kneeling Woman/Legend	10.00	20.00	35.00	125.00
13. Liberty Head Left/ Legend "Mint Drop"	1.50	3.50	7.50	25.00
14. Man Standing Left/ Jackass	1.50	3.50	8.00	27.50
15. Man in Chest/Jackass	1.50	3.00	6.50	22.50
16. Pig Running Left/ Bust Over Legend	1.50	3.00	6.50	22.50
17. Turtle Right/Jackass	1.50	3.00	6.50	22.50
18. Liberty Head Left/ Legend "Not One Cent"	1.50	3.00	6.50	22.50

	Good	Fine	Ex. Fine	Unc.
19. Liberty Head Left/ Legend "May Tenth"...............	2.00	4.00	7.50	30.00
20. Phoenix/Legend	1.50	3.00	6.00	20.00
20. Ship/Shipwreck........................	1.50	3.00	6.50	22.50
22. Shipwreck/Man in Chest	1.50	3.00	6.50	25.00
23. Ship/Legend............................	1.50	3.00	6.50	22.50
24. Ship/Liberty Head	7.50	15.00	35.00	75.00
25. Half-Cent................................	25.00	40.00	85.00	250.00

50.
CIVIL WAR
TOKENS

These are copper or brass tokens, privately struck during the years 1860-66, ostensibly to help alleviate the shortage of Federal cents caused by hoarding. Although they were approximately the size of an Indian Head cent, many were underweight. As they were sold to merchants by their manufacturers at a discount from face value, this underweight condition is to be expected—war profiteers existing then as now. Several hundred varieties of the patriotic kind exist, and prices are listed for the major types. Many thousands of varieties exist for the merchants' or advertising types, and they fall beyond our scope (values for common advertising Civil War tokens—Good $1.00; Fine $1.75; Ex. Fine $2.50; Unc. $5.00.)

Type	Good	Fine	Ex. Fine	Unc.
1. Liberty Head Left	1.00	1.75	2.75	5.00
2. Liberty Head Right	1.25	2.00	3.00	6.00
3. Indian Head Left	1.00	1.75	2.50	5.00
4. Washington Head Left	5.00	10.00	22.50	50.00
5. Washington Head Right	1.50	3.00	5.00	10.00
6. Lincoln Head Left	2.50	6.00	10.00	25.00
7. Lincoln Head Right	3.00	7.50	15.00	40.00
8. McClellan Head Left	1.50	2.50	4.00	10.00
9. McClellan Head Right	1.50	2.50	4.00	10.00
10. Franklin Head Left	5.00	15.00	35.00	100.00
11. Franklin Head Right	3.50	9.00	25.00	75.00
12. Flying Eagle Right	10.00	25.00	60.00	250.00
13. Flying Eagle Left	9.00	22.50	50.00	150.00
14. Upright Eagle	7.50	20.00	35.00	100.00
15. Eagle on Shield	1.00	1.75	2.50	5.00
16. Cannon	1.50	2.50	3.50	9.00
17. Man on Horseback	1.50	2.50	4.00	10.00
18. Flag	1.00	1.75	2.50	5.00
19. Ship	1.50	3.50	5.00	12.00
20. Walking Man	1.50	3.50	5.00	12.00
21. Scroll	10.00	25.00	75.00	300.00
22. Wreath	1.00	1.75	2.50	5.00

51.
COINS OF
HAWAII

There was an issue of dimes, quarters, half-dollars and dollars struck by King Kalakaua in 1883; these were manufactured at the San Francisco Mint, although no mintmark appears on the pieces. There was also an issue of cents in 1847, bearing the bust of Kamehameha III and the legend "Apuni Hawaii, Hapa Haneri". (Beware of Spurious Specimens, which have an unnatural golden appearance.)

	Good	Fine	Ex. Fine	Unc.	Proof
1847 Cent...........................	85.00	175.00	300.00	750.00	—
1883 Dime.........................	10.00	25.00	175.00	750.00	4,000.00
1883 Quarter......................	10.00	20.00	60.00	150.00	4,000.00
1883 Half-Dollar................	35.00	60.00	140.00	700.00	4,500.00
1883 Dollar.......................	110.00	210.00	550.00	4,000.00	6,000.00

52.
Philippine
Islands

From 1903 to 1945 the coinage of the Philippines was under the sovereignty of the United States of America. Types are uniform, as follows:

$^1/_2$¢ , 1¢ , 5¢ - Man leaning on anvil, "Filipinas" below/Eagle on shield, "United States of America" around.

10¢ , 20¢ , 50¢ , 1 Peso - Standing female, "Filipinas" below/ "United States of America" around eagle on shield.

Prices are for most common dates.

Type		Fine	Ex. Fine	Unc.	Proof
Half Centavo	1903-08	.50	1.50	5.00	20.00
One Centavo	1903-36	.50	1.50	5.00	20.00
One Centavo	1937-44	.10	.25	.50	20.00
Five Centavos	1903-28	.50	1.50	5.00	20.00
Five Centavos	1930-45	.10	.25	.50	—
Ten Centavos	1903-06	.75	2.50	10.00	25.00
Ten Centavos	1907-45	.25	.50	1.00	25.00
Twenty Centavos	1903-06	1.00	3.00	10.00	30.00
Twenty Centavos	1907-45	.50	.75	1.50	75.00
Fifty Centavos	1903-06	3.50	9.00	22.50	40.00
Fifty Centavos	1907-45	3.00	4.00	6.00	100.00
One Peso	1903-06	12.00	18.00	30.00	75.00
One Peso	1907-12	8.00	15.00	25.00	175.00

Commemoratives

	Fine	Ex. Fine	Unc.
1936 50 Centavos, Facing Busts	12.50	35.00	50.00
1936 Peso, Murphy & Quezon	35.00	70.00	110.00
1936 Peso, Roosevelt & Quezon	35.00	70.00	110.00

Note: After World War II, many hundreds of these commemoratives were dredged up from Manila Bay, where they had lain since their dumping at the time of the Japanese invasion. These pieces bear the scars of long immersion in saltwater—pits, pockmarks, corrosion, etc.—and are worth very little as collectors pieces.